Zarathustra Stone

Other books by Mark Anderson

Diamythologōmen
Thinking Life: A Philosophical Fiction
Moby-Dick *as Philosophy: Plato-Melville-Nietzsche*

Zarathustra Stone

Friedrich Nietzsche in Sils-Maria
August, 1881

Mark Anderson

S.Ph.

S.Ph. Press
Nashville, TN

Copyright © 2016 by S.Ph. Press

All rights reserved. No part of this publication may be reproduced or utilized in any form or by any means without permission in writing from the publisher.

ISBN-13: 978-0-9967725-3-2
ISBN-10: 0-9967725-3-7

Library of Congress Control Number: 2016913062

Cover photograph by Mark Anderson
Design by Mark Anderson and Tim Duggan

www.sphpress.com

↺ ↺ ↺ ↺ ↺

8 August, 1881
Sils-Maria, Switzerland

5:30 am – 7:30 am

The professor awoke from a disturbing dream, shaken and disoriented, a warm thickness pulsing behind his right eye. Instinctively he raised a hand to massage his temple's tender skin, careful not to move his head. He had learned from years of hard experience that even a minor agitation could quicken the dull throbbing into a migraine, pitiless with vertigo and vomiting. He opened his left eye slowly, narrowly, and scanned the dark room through a haze of blurred vision. The first pale light of dawn glowed against the window in the opposite wall, a muted indigo emerging from night, lingering outside shy, reserved, not yet bold to penetrate the pane. Day was breaking but the sun itself was still obscured behind the encircling mountains, thickly wooded, tangled shadows, and higher up above the tree-line, frozen and snow.

 He curled his feet and clinched his toes beneath the blankets, pulled the linen sheet over his neck and tucked it under his chin. The air beyond the woolen quilt was cold. The professor was cold himself, yet he perspired. Wiping the sweat from his brow with a cuff of his night-shirt, he lay still, closed his heavy eye, and retreated into himself, turning away from corporeal pressures to pursue the dispersing fragments of his dream. At first he recalled no content, only sensed a mood. But soon the images reappeared, not as a return of the dream itself, but rather as a memory of the dream. A musical metaphor rang in his mind: his dream as a variation on a theme he had dreamt as a child, not long after the premature death of his father.

The professor's father, Carl Ludwig, had served as pastor of a Lutheran church in the small Prussian village of Röcken, where his son Friedrich—known to family and friends as Fritz—enjoyed a bucolic childhood of meadows and sky, hedgerows, streams, and ponds. As a boy he gamboled and played outdoors for hours every day, chasing clouds, climbing trees, picking flowers and skipping stones. Inside the home were other fascinations, fully as alluring as the natural world: the pastor's study lined with shelves of books; his maps and prints stacked on a table in the light of a south-facing window; his desk an organized clutter of dictionaries, notebooks, and manuscript sermons in various states of revision. Often as his father worked, Fritz sat quietly in front of his desk, a large book open on his lap, studying the pastor's concentrated brow and striving to mirror the look on his own face while reading or pretending to read.

As the eldest child, Fritz occupied a special place in his father's affections, and he in turn cherished his father, admired him and longed to be like him. The pastor was a serious soul, quiet and sometimes even somber; but he beamed with a lively cheerfulness when playing the piano, which he did often and with accomplishment, laughing and winking at his son as he played.

In earnest imitation of his father, Fritz learned early to read and write, to love God and treasure the Bible. He marveled too at the other volumes in the family library, the mysteries they contained; and he pored over the maps and prints, fantasizing distant lands and ancient civilizations. Later he would compose precocious poems and learn to play the piano, delighting especially in whimsical improvisations.

In short, Fritz's world was an idyllic blend of fantasy and nature. Pure naive unbounded wonder. Intellect and self-discipline too.

Fritz played well with his younger sister, Elizabeth, whom he called Lisbeth, and sometimes, affectionately, Lama. Two years her elder, he assumed a child's responsibility for her well-being and protection, and he fulfilled with dutiful zeal the role of fraternal custodian. No playing on the ice; no chasing bees; bundle up; scrub your face; obey mama and papa. He held her hand when they walked together outdoors, sat beside her at night on a rug in the glow of the hearth-fire, their father reading stories aloud, their mother reciting ancient songs and nursery rhymes. The annual seasons came for the children and went. Laughing winter sleigh rides carted them into budding fields of spring, beyond which blossomed exuberant summer frolicking, bare feet through to soft autumn sweaters.

Then came the gift of new life, a third child, babbling baby Joseph, the cynosure of the family constellation. His parents attended lovingly to his every need; his siblings marveled at the smallness of him, played with him as with a favorite doll. By nature the child cherished the attention. He delighted in company and rarely cried; he seemed almost laughter incarnate. His blue eyes were curious, joyful, lunar-round and gleaming. His soft skin somehow radiated light, and it shone more brightly every day. He suckled; he grew; he rolled over onto his stomach; he crawled.

Fritz followed little Joseph everywhere, enraptured with fascination and love. He dragged Lama behind him too, lecturing her on his every observation of the baby's behavior, and teaching her lessons of kindness and concern.

The sunshine of the family's happiness glowed with a mellow warmth, their little world spinning in radiating waves of divine beneficence. But then in an instant late in the summer of Fritz's fourth birthday, their celestial security was inexplicably withdrawn, and their lives were forever altered. At work in his study early one evening, in the sunset of a pleasantly idle afternoon, the pastor was seized by a paralytic fit that shook and stunned him and left him unconscious for days. He recovered in time, but the seizures recurred, then assailed him more often with escalating intensity. For months he cycled from lethargy to rage, from clarity of thought to stammering bewilderment, from vigor to helpless incapacitation. He lost his sight.

Nine months following the initial attack the pastor was gone—a pregnancy of pain unto death. Despite the fiction the family concocted to the effect that he had fallen and hit his head, the symptoms of degenerative mental instability were unmistakable. The local physician pronounced the cause of death 'softening of the brain.' He was only thirty-six.

Throughout the night of his father's death, Fritz overheard his sister whimpering, "Father is dead!" In the bedroom with her mother, crying, "Father is dead!" For months she wandered as if in a daze, aimless and fey. "Father is dead!"

Fritz himself was deeply distraught by the loss of his father, though perhaps he externalized it less. Interiorly, however, he felt abandoned, cruelly set to wandering alone in the dark, as if an enormous guiding sun had set. He was far too young to comprehend the significance, or even the fact, of the loneliness and melancholy that settled into his bones at the time, but he was penetrated to the marrow.

The changes in his psychic state emerged obliquely, through unusual patterns of thought and strange dreams, as when a few months after his father's death he dreamt he awoke at midnight to the sound of church-bells tolling plaintively, then climbed from bed and crept over to peek through his bedroom window. Rubbing his eyes, he looked down into the graveyard beside the chapel, where a heaving mist circulated among the tombstones. Suddenly a rumbling shock, as from distant thunder, and a pyramidal mound of soil atop a grave gave way, collapsing into the earth. Then from the chasm a figure emerged, neither crawling nor climbing but rising weightless without a sound. This was his father, or the insubstantial ghost of his father, or somehow both. The tolling of the church-bells rang more deeply, reverberating ominously. Fritz trembled but resisted the urge to avert his eyes, and he watched in awe and dread as the phantasm glided over the lawn onto the wooden porch below his window. The front door rattled in the foyer beneath his room. The stairs beyond his bedroom door groaned and creaked. Then, silence.

A moment flashed before him hot and bright, an eye-blink lightning-quick, simultaneously creeping as a ponderous eternity, and the pastor emerged on the lawn cradling a bundle in his arms. Fritz heard mournful moaning sounds but could not identify the source. Perhaps they came from his own constricted throat. But in fact the strains drifted up from the swaddled thing in his father's embrace.

As the figure descended again into the grave, the moaning ceased, the twelfth resounding toll trailed off into silence, and an infinite darkness descended.

The following morning Fritz slept much later than usual, and he might have slept even longer still had he not been awakened by his mother's cries. Hurrying from his room he discovered her across the hall, on her knees beside his brother's cradle. The child was shivering, sweating, moaning and jerking in twisted contortions. His sister ran through the house in a panic, wailing and tearing her hair. The doctor was summoned, but his eager ministrations were in vain. The child died that very day.

Young Fritz never spoke to his mother of his dream-premonition, but the mood induced by his unaccountable prescience colored his thought-world in minatory hues that haunted him the rest of his life.

***

The professor lay in bed reflecting on this enigmatic episode of his youth, quiet, unmoving, the room still more dark than not. A rooster crowed somewhere in the distance. He attended then to the fact that this morning's dream had not precisely mirrored the original. In this recent variation the ghostly apparition had emerged from the grave with a bundle already in its arms. Then entering the house it deposited the thing in the realm of the living, then retreated into the ground alone. Moreover, in this variation the figures involved were not the professor's father and brother. They were both him.

Downstairs his landlord returned from hunting chamois, heavy treading on hardwood floors, the muffled crunch of snow and cold and ice-stiff clothes. He permitted the distant rumbling to penetrate the theater of his mind, infusing every echo with the mood evoked by the scenes playing out in the spotlight of his imagination. He was thinking of his father and baby brother, of himself, too, himself as infant and adult, adult and infant, an identity cycling through oppositional states, dying yet reborn, reanimated, episodically recurring. "Like unto leaves is the breed of men," he recited his schoolboy Homer from memory, rolling the hexameters over his tongue. "The wind scatters leaves on the ground, but the forest flourishing blooms, and the season of spring returns."

Preparing now to open his eyes and throw off his bedsheets, the professor inwardly inspected the condition of his head, his shoulders and spine as well. He was neither comfortable nor completely lucid, but he had managed to evade the long-toothed predator, agonia stalking. He felt well enough, perhaps even bright, with the exception of a fog of melancholia exuded by his dream. Rolling from bed he wrapped a robe around his nightclothes and crossed the room to sit down at a little table under the window. From the sky he read the promise of a day bright blue with a welcoming sun, comfortable with only an edge of chill to the west on Lake Sils in the morning, sufficiently warm by afternoon for a walk north to Lake Silvaplana, on whose far shore there stood an enormous pyramidal stone that had lured him to the site on every one of the past eleven days. "Like a Siren," he thought. "And today my twelfth visit. A midday and a zenith." Then he whispered, as if in reply to a question put to him by the stone itself, "Yes."

Prior to the recent fortnight of good weather, the professor had suffered throughout July from the valley's unseasonably high temperatures and frequent storms. He disliked, even feared, cumulonimbus clouds, convinced as he was that meteorological electrical charges upset the precarious balance of his nervous system. The ceaseless rain, high winds, thunder and lightning booming for days on end, had incapacitated him. He lay in bed most all day long contending with headaches so intense his body writhed with rhythmic waves of pressure and release. During the rare intermittent periods of bearable pain, he lay on his back with his hands folded across his abdomen, eyes closed, head still and spine straight, concentrating on each inhalation and exhalation of breath, attempting with as little exertion as possible to relax, as if he could hide from the prowling pain, which might pass on to some other unfortunate prey. Inevitably, however, the beast sniffed him out, attacking first as oppressive pressure in the head, then as radiating bursts of heat, and finally as the sharp piercings of canines and claws tearing into his brain.

Often in the course of these seizure-fits the orbicularis muscle of his right eye contracted so tightly he was physically unable to relax it, simply could not unclench the lid for hours. And when finally the flexion slackened, his eye was no good for seeing; it registered only milky swimming after-images of obscure apparitions.

When his attacks intensified to this extreme, the professor's every attempt to lie still was ineffective. He rolled over on one side, then lay on his back, shifted to his opposite side, then turned onto his stomach. Sometimes he spun in his sheets this way for hours, endlessly uncomfortable. When especially desperate, he bent his legs and hugged his knees, but this reversion to fetal form only aroused the predator's bloodlust. Internal contractions agitated his bowels, and his stomach pumped black bile and phlegm up through his esophagus and mouth in retching bursts of vomiting spasms, grating his throat and soiling his tongue. So extreme was the pressure of these episodes that his head filled with blood almost to bursting, his eyes grotesquely bulged, and sweat, saliva, and tears squeezed through his every pore, as if the full store of unbound elements within were desperate to escape the awful interior theater of war.

During the worst hours of these attacks the professor could neither see, nor hear, nor speak, nor generate a coherent thought. He was all and only organism, uncategorizable animal, malfunctioning meat. To observe him twisted in sheets soaked through with sweat, his upper body hanging lifeless from the bed, his head draining viscous liquids into a pail of vomitous waste—to see him thus might well convince even the most cynical skeptic to dread the wrath of an angry god.

As debilitating as these episodes were, the professor was grimly accustomed to the pain. He had been afflicted for years. Just two years earlier, in the summer of 1879, the regular recurrence of his fits had forced him to resign his post as Professor of Philology at the University of Basel. "My headaches have so intensified that I can hardly bear them any longer," he wrote to the President of the university board. "My seizures persist anywhere from two to six days," he explained, "and my doctor has informed me yet again that my eyesight continues to worsen. Indeed, even the briefest session of reading or writing induces unbearable pain." He had, he concluded, regretfully determined "that I can no longer function competently as an academic, for I cannot fulfill even the most rudimentary of my responsibilities as a professor." In December of that year he wrote in a letter to a friend that he had suffered "118 days of the *most serious* disorders of the head and nerves." One of every three days suffering, and he was only thirty-four years old.

Standing up from the table the professor removed his robe and nightshirt, stepped over to the bureau on the opposite wall, and observed his reflection in the mirror. The skin around his right eye was discolored, most likely, he reasoned, from muscular strain. He poured fresh water from a pitcher into the porcelain bowl on the washstand, then he rinsed his hands and scrubbed his face, shoulders, and chest, then drained the remaining water over his head. His body shivered from the chill, but he inhaled deeply, held his breath, and concentrated to still the palpitations. From his youth he had regularly bathed in cold water, even in wintry streams whenever he could, as an exercise in discipline and a genial antagonism to the bitterness of ice. Thus he inured himself to pain.

After drying off with a large towel, he checked his eye again in the mirror. It appeared normal now, clean and relaxed like the rest of his face.

Below the base of the mirror, collected atop the bureau, stood several small bottles of pills and clear liquids, neatly arranged and labelled by hand. The professor travelled with a makeshift pharmacy of stimulants and opiates, all of which he acquired by way of prescriptions he wrote himself and signed with his official title, 'Dr.' He was particularly reliant on the chloral hydrate he employed to induce sleep, which eluded him especially during his worst bouts of illness. From time to time he took the drug even when he felt well, but then the doses kept him awake and, worse, they sometimes produced terrifying spells of kaleidoscopic hallucinations.

When the professor first experienced these strange visual phenomena, he panicked from fear of impending madness and death, his father's dreadful fate. Yet he persisted in medicating himself, not only from the conviction that he managed his disorder better than any one of the score of doctors he had consulted over the years, but also because he valued the extraordinary perspectives through which he viewed the world when intoxicated. He craved the Dionysian insight, though usually he suffered terribly after the fact. Therefore he restricted his intake to occasions of especially urgent need.

The professor had done without his 'medicines' for nearly two weeks now, and a thin layer of dust had settled over the bottles and phials. He wiped them clean with a corner of his towel, smiling at his recent run of good health. Then, after hanging the towel on a stand beside the bureau, he removed a pair of dark trousers and a white button shirt from the closet, and dressed.

The world outside his window was taking on color in the light, but as it was still early, he sat down again at the table and reached for one of the many notebooks scattered before him. He held it up close to his left eye, straining to read. Then he took up his thick, wire-rimmed glasses, laid the notebook open on the table and turned through several pages, pausing now and then to lean back in his chair, his face turned toward the ceiling, eyes closed. After several minutes of alternately reading and reflecting in this manner, he pushed the notebook aside and picked up another, smaller, notebook, of a size convenient for carrying in his pocket. He opened it to a page near the center and studied his most recent notes, crossing out or revising infelicities of expression. Then, replacing the notebook on the table beside several freshly sharpened pencils, he turned in his chair, looked again through the window at the brightening sky, and gave himself over to ruminating on the significance of his dream.

He was struck in particular by his appearing in place of his father, a dead man returning to life, and delivering himself as an infant to life, all this under the gaze of himself as a child, and all *this* as dreamt by himself as an adult very nearly the age at which his father died. For years he had feared he too would die at thirty-six, and as he had only just buried the date, he still felt uneasy. So perhaps it made sense, his appearing in the dream as his father. But why, he wondered, why should he carry himself as an infant rather than his infant brother, and why bear the child up out of the grave rather than draw him down into it?

A sudden sounding of movement and voices downstairs indicated that Frau Durisch was awake and about. The children would likely remain in bed until the sun was well up. The professor checked the weather through the window one last time, then he collected his small notebook and a pencil from the table, crossed the room, and lifting his jacket from a hook on the back of the door, he slipped the items into his left pocket. After donning the jacket he squeezed this pocket to feel for the notebook and pencil inside, a compulsion he'd indulged for years—as his mind was constantly active, he dreaded the thought of his best ideas drifting away into the ether; therefore he made a point of always having writing materials to hand. He reached for his pocket again after leaving the room, pressing to feel each specific item inside. Then he descended the central staircase, stepping lightly on the old wooden treads, careful not to disturb the still slumbering children.

"Morning, Herr Professor," Gian Durisch rang out as the professor entered the kitchen. "An egg yolk and biscuit for you, sir, before you leave? And tea, of course, as usual?"

"Yes, thank you," and the professor sat down at the modest kitchen table. "And good morning to you, sir. How went your hunting this morning?" He smiled at Frau Durisch as her husband held up his display of game, and he asked the pair about their children. Frau Durisch cut into a loaf of bread while speaking of her daughter's studies, her son's pranks and outdoor adventures, musing on their divergent personalities.

"Ah, Frau Durisch," the professor sighed at a memory stirring. "In your words I hear a description of my own divided character. I was a serious student myself as a child, but also something of a rascal. I recall one summer when a dour old scholar passed a holiday in our town. I had the reputation of a 'little saint,' as my classmates liked to call me. And I was, too. But from time to time some mad force overcame me and I misbehaved, never maliciously, mind you, but not quite innocently either. In any case, this particular old man carried an umbrella for protection from the sun, and when one afternoon I saw him resting on a bench beneath a tree, with his umbrella hanging from the back of his seat, some devil put it in my mind to creep up and drop a handful of pebbles inside, so that when he opened the umbrella the stones would rain down on his head. I must say it was a great success. Ha! I laugh to recall it."

And he did laugh, too, shaking his head. But when Frau Durisch urged him to continue, laughing herself, he hesitated and closed his eyes. "A great success indeed," he said. "I observed the event from beside a tree not far from the scene of my crime. As the pebbles pelted the old man's head and shoulders, he exhibited no signs of anger; he rather displayed an expression of dejected resignation. Then he rubbed his scalp and turned to scan the area for the miscreant responsible. Our eyes met as he turned, and in his gaze I read a look of profound sadness, as of a friendless man passing through life without love, devoid even of the hope of love. Of course he could not have known that I was the culprit, but through his eyes I saw myself as one in a long line of his tormentors, from childhood to old age, harassed by thoughtless fools who drove an erstwhile merry child to curse his life and wish himself well out of it. I turned and ran from the man, ran crying all the way home. I wept through the night too, and although my mother pleaded with me, I refused to explain myself. Oh, I can still see the world-weary aspect of that old man's face! In fact, I sometimes seem to see it in my mirror..."

"But forgive me," the professor started, blinking his eyes emerging from his cave of recollection. "Forgive me, Frau Durisch, this is no talk for breakfast before a bright summer's day."

Frau Durisch smiled and handed the professor a thick slice of bread. "Well," she said, "you really should forgive yourself your childish misdeeds. You meant no harm, I'm sure. And after all, every one of us has done such silly things to friends and strangers alike. '*Siamo poveri mortali*,' as they say. Poor mortals indeed."

The professor returned Frau Durisch's smile then spoke at length of happy memories of his youth, laughing and stirring the Durisches to laugh until they forgot his earlier melancholy tale. He sipped his tea while reminiscing and wrapped his bread in a handkerchief, carefully folding the corners to envelop the slice, which he placed in his right jacket pocket. Then he stood up from the table and said, "A delicious meal, as always," with a nod of the head to Frau Durisch. "Thank you, thank you both."

"You're most welcome, of course," Frau Durisch replied, then remarked before he turned to leave that he appeared especially robust this morning. "So good to see you maintaining a healthy constitution," she added, "and for nearly two weeks now. Last month was hard on you, I know."

"More than hard," her husband interjected. "Very nearly humanly unbearable, I would say. One would think you somehow more than human, Herr Professor, seeing you of late so fit and cheerful."

"Indeed, Herr Durisch," the professor replied with a shy, almost inward smile. "Cheerfulness is dear to me, for it is essential to my recovery, to my cure. And one might say my very life hangs always in the balance between cheerfulness and death."

Then, reaching fully into his jacket pocket to finger his notebook and pencil, he bid the couple good morning and walked down the hall toward the front door.

7:30 am

The professor stood outside with his back to the door of the Durisches' house, lingering on the wood-plank porch to admire the grandeur of the towering peak across the way. Mt. Lagrev, granite grey and pine green, and at its summit streaked with tracks of snow, swept up soaring from the meadows on the far side of the valley. The Durisch house was overloomed by several such peaks, for the little village of Sils-Maria nestled near the southern end of the Upper Engadine valley, a long, level, verdant trough running north between the wooded bases of the Albula and Bernina ranges of the Western Rhaetian Alps.

The professor had arrived in the Engadine from Italy early in July, travelling west by train from Recoaro to Milan, then north beside Lake Como to Chiavenna, whence inside a post-chaise carriage he traversed the long incline road into Switzerland, climbing between the Oberhalbstein and Bregaglia ranges, then ascending the steep, switchback pass-road toward Maloja, six thousand feet above the sea.

Little more than a dispersed assemblage of rustic homes, a post office, and a station for changing carriage-horses, Maloja occupied the southernmost district of the Engadine valley. Situated on a rise above the southern shore of Lake Sils, the area was ideal for a lonely hiker to rest and enjoy the view, or to nap in the grass to the gentle sounds of the waves on the lake below.

Two-thousand feet above Maloja, brooding between the haughty peaks of Grevasalvas and Lunghin, the melancholic Lunghinsee flowed off as the watershed of the Inn River, whose winding course to the Danube, and thence to the Black Sea, ran from Maloja through the whole of the Engadine, filling in turn the lakes of Sils, Silvaplana, Champfèr, and St. Moritz at the northernmost end of the valley.

The professor often expressed his fondness for mountains 'with eyes,' by which he meant *with lakes*. The Engadine was as a birth-twin to his spirit.

Lake Sils, the largest of the Engadine's major lakes, spanned the three miles between Maloja and Sils-Maria, pinched in the middle by a wooded outcrop at the base of Mt. Materdell on its western shore, on the eastern side by the roundly protruding meadows of Isola, a huddled collection of farmers' dwellings, vegetable gardens, and livestock watering troughs at the base Mt. da la Margna. Cattle grazed on Isola's marshy shore every afternoon, their hollow bells clanging the descent of the sun behind the peaks across the lake.

From the northern shore of Lake Sils, a short walk from the Durisches' house in Sils proper, the densely-wooded Chastè peninsula jutted its crooked finger far into the water. Locals moored small fishing-boats in a bobbing row along its eastern bank; mother doe led their fawns to feed in the shade of the trees hard by the shore; and tuft-eared red squirrel scurried after pine seeds in the dense foliage. Wild but walkable, the peninsula's interior reminded the professor of a forest scene meticulously reproduced on an opera-house stage, a fantastical realm for a peripatetic pondering man to experience authentic feelings of isolation, with only birdsong and the murmurings of water for company, while remaining near to human things, the bustling world of ideas.

The narrow shaded walking-paths that wound around Chastè, cooled by the winds blowing off the lake, alternately descended into sheltered coves, where rounded stones reposed beneath translucent waters, and climbed toward a broad central rise on which were scattered the ruined foundations of an ancient Roman fort. Hand-hewn benches of local pine, placed by the villagers here and there on level stretches of the trails, gave access to lake and mountain views.

Mornings when the wind was low and the temperature mild, the professor was accustomed to rest on a bench at the southern end of Chastè, gazing down on the glassy water below, abandoning his thoughts to sink into the depths, there to dart and sport among the shadowy forms of extraordinary creatures and concepts. Or tracing the outline of the mountains rising at angles on either side of the pass beyond Maloja, the sky between a shining blue infinity, he rose to sublime heights of intellect unattained by prior contemplative visitors to the site, including even the ancient haruspex, encamped among the Roman legions, praying and pouring libations to his gods.

When in these moods the professor could almost imagine the lake a dreamscape of his own invention, or the work of a divine painter, its smooth surface a serene unblinking eye trained every day on the sun, every night on the stars. On blustery afternoons, when the winds whipped up through the Maloja pass and disturbed the waters' contemplative calm, the lake itself transformed into the artist: the water under the rustling wind flashed with multicolored facets leaping at angles from the waves, a fragmented mirror moving beneath reflected sky, and the surrounding mountains imaged on its surface danced kaleidoscopically, as from the brush of an early Impressionist.

So taken was the professor with Chastè that he fancied erecting a hermitage on the site. The area around the Roman fortifications was sufficiently level, natural stores of wood to burn for heat grew round in lush profusion, and the lake itself was suitable for bathing. Most inviting of all was the promise of solitude. Some of the older local women took their morning exercise in the nearby meadows; and summer guests explored the peninsula itself, but most kept to the lower paths near the water's edge, or hiked up to the mid-level ridges on the southern side overlooking the lake. Few braved the steep, rocky trail leading up to the highest central point. Therefore, the professor thought, he might occupy his hilltop shelter more or less unmolested.

He had shared his idea with the Durisches once over breakfast, but the couple were dubious. His practical landlord wondered aloud about property rights, and Frau Durisch feared for his safety alone in a makeshift hut assailed eight months of the year by wind, rain, and prodigious drifts of snow. They were sympathetic to his plight, and gentle with him as always, but they made a point of discouraging the venture.

The professor acknowledged the impracticality of his living alone in the woods, but he could not put out of his mind the dream of leading a hermit's life, if only for a time as an experiment in treating his illness. He had taken many a so-called 'cure' at spas throughout Europe, bathing in the hot-springs, drinking bitter mineral water, enduring massages and moonshine lectures on the benefits of salt or the dangers of fruits and greens. In the end he always came to the same conclusion: no one knew his illness as intimately as he did himself. Therefore he alone could cure it, if indeed it could be cured. What he needed was solitude and the tranquility of a quiet routine, but in the vicinity of friends or relatives to whom he could turn for assistance whenever he required company or care.

Two summers earlier he had nearly realized just such a project, having all but secured a lease on a tower in the medieval wall around the town in which his mother and sister lived. These towers having originally been equipped for occupancy by sentries, a well-preserved turret with the appropriate modifications would have accommodated all his needs. The largest were outfitted with small stone fire-pits, basins for washing, and outdoor latrines. There were water-wells too, some still in use. For his part, he would have only to supply a cot, a small desk and a chair, and of course he would bring a chest for storing clothes and his numerous books and notebooks. He preferred to inhabit a section of the wall farthest from the crowded districts, out near the lanes that ran through the fields among the farmers' homesteads. There he could cultivate a small patch of land on the sunny side of the wall, and so tend to his nourishment in accord with his own idiosyncratic ideas regarding physiological well-being.

The hermit's life would be good for his spirit, too, withdrawn as he would be from commerce with a modern world whose decline into decadence burdened his mind and upset his stomach more grievously every year, sometimes almost nauseating him. He would live as best he could as an ancient recluse, an archaic Hellenic eccentric in the tradition of Heraclitus, aloof from the news of empire and the chatter of officious Ephesians, a pagan ascetic dedicated to nature, health, and the pursuit of high-spirited cheerfulness.

In the end nothing came of either one of the professor's designs for a radical monastic cure, nothing anyway apart from the joy of imagining himself in their glow, a joy that was pleasant in itself and which also infused his mood and colored his self-conception: he could live as a hermit wherever his residence happened to be from season to season; and he could be a gardener too—was he not already the noblest type of gardener, breeding and cultivating ideas of a species heretofore unknown to the world?

Such were the more mundane of the thoughts that occupied the professor's mind as he wandered the wooded footpaths of Chastè; they occurred to him especially when he picked through the Roman ruins under the morning sun, broken shafts of light filtering through the larches, or sat on the stones imagining his way into the minds of the ancients who had sat there centuries before, so far from home, from their gods, so high in the mountains—precisely as he sat there himself, far above the world his contemporaries knew, or thought they knew.

To the northwest of Chastè the Inn emerged from Lake Sils to flow toward Lake Silvaplana, meandering beside the main valley road along the western perimeter of the Sils meadows. Watered by the Inn and the Fedacla, a river flowing down from the Fex Valley behind Mt. Corvatsch to the east, the five hundred acres of meadowland were lush with a variety of flora, shading from the pale greens of foxtail and knotgrass to the darker tones of woodrush and black alpine sedge.

Feathergrass moving in the wind streaked the meadows with shifting highlights of pale goldenrod, and sweeping lanes of alpine bluegrass rolled in waves of silvery purple.

When the professor first arrived in Sils, the meadows shone with a variety of yellow flowers. Dandelions and the delicate buttercup predominated, and here and there the bulbous globe-flower balanced atop its long stem, resembling to the professor's eye a small scoop of the finest Milanese limone gelato. Yellow poppies, cinquefoil, and common bird's-foot trefoil grew everywhere around, as did the bright auricula and the yellow rock-rose. From a distance he could hardly see the green base of the meadows, so thoroughly carpeted were the fields by layered shades of yellow.

By mid-July the dandelions had matured and dispersed on the wind, the globe-flowers were slowly melting in the sun, and a multicolored profusion of blooms sprang up among the remaining stands of buttercups, poppies, and rock-rose. First to appear was the tall bistort; growing in expansive curving lanes, the soft fuchsia swabs washed the meadow in mellow tints of purple and pink. Fragile shoots of alpine orchids followed, their buds exquisite gems mounted in stacks of violet and white. Swaying in the wind, they brushed the bistort like coquettes in cotton summer dresses, shy but desiring attention.

Later, lavender blooms of Geranium sylvaticum sprouted in the shade of trees from which the soft blue bells of alpine clematis hung. Pink primroses blossomed beside white anemones and clumps of pastel alpine rose. And clusters of the diminutive forget-me-not, powder blue with tiny central discs of yellow or white, peeked out from tangled thickets of green.

Come August, white daisies were everywhere in flower, splaying their creamy petals; by the thousands they formed wide channels coursing through the meadows in bending streams. Their yellow daisy cousins spread out beside them, scattering over the fields a luminous solar glow.

Butterflies flitted crazily over the sprawling Sils meadows, alighting on flowers, feeding then fluttering away. The twittering of birds and the warm hum of crickets moved on the wind. And now and then the lazy shadow of a roving cloud drifted overhead, muting the meadows' colors and cooling the air. The languid atmospherics infused the days with an aura of relaxed tranquility, as if nature were napping and reviewing in dreams her fondest secret wishes.

The professor delighted in the Engadine's meadows, the flowers in particular. For years he had cultivated an arctic intellectual severity, which he likened to the aloof austerities of mountain summits, the raw brutality of ice grinding into high peaks. But his supreme ambition was to combine a stern intellectual conscience with the gay good-will of a laughing dancer and poet. When he went into the mountains, it was not to scale high frozen peaks and glower on the valley below from among dark clouds; it was rather to wander through wild woods and meadows, thinking; to sit on the banks of the lakes, writing; to admire the sky and inhale the bracing air. He picked flowers from the fields to display in a vase in his room, changed the water every morning. The professor was, in brief, as delicate as grave, and the Sils meadows resonated with his light-heartedness, brightening his mood, and made of him on the best of days a lover, a joker, a fool and playful sage.

Running north through the meadows away from the populated area of Sils, a wide dirt and gravel path approached the southern bank of Lake Silvaplana, worn from the passage of transport wagons hauling loggers from the village onto the forested flanks of Corvatsch. These lumbermen stacked felled trees to cure on the southern shore of the lake, in the sun in the path of the Maloja winds. Thin ribbons of yellow, white, and blue tied to the stumps of lopped-off branches indicated ownership, fluttering in the breeze like wildflowers.

On the southern shore of Silvaplana the loggers' track, branching left, narrowed into a walking-trail leading west to the mouths of the Fedacla and Inn rivers. To the right a winding path tracked the eastern shoreline of the lake, at first close by the bank, then veering away into the trees atop a broad plateau, descending again beside the water, and curving finally into the meadows beyond the northern shore.

Lake Silvaplana was wilder than Lake Sils, its atmosphere pervaded by a numinous electricity. Even the flowers in the meadow on its far shore were moody, dusky with bands of red sorrel clustered around masses of alpine dock, blood-drop sanguisorba throughout, and blazing patches of golden hawk's-beard, the darker hues crowding the yellows and whites. The Maloja winds that rippled the surface of Lake Sils, or at most churned up innocuous rounded waves, regularly gathered force above the open expanse of the Sils meadows to roil the waters of Lake Silvaplana with turbulent gales.

On the far side of the lake, in the northeast corner at the base of pudgy Mt. Surlej, the pyramidal stone that had drawn the professor into its presence for each of the past eleven days rose twelve feet high, angling up in rough granite lines from a broad square base to a thick rounded peak. Apart from the surrounding mountains, no geological feature in the area resembled this stone, which stood alone as if it had fallen to earth in a distant millennium from a realm beyond the stars, a supra-cosmic Egypt whose pyramids sprang from the soil as natural formations.

The atmosphere around the stone affected the professor as if it pulsed with steady emanations that penetrated his skin, transferring to his nerves its excited energy. Whenever he approached the area, his mind flamed with the promise of insight. What this insight might be, he did not know, but he sensed it moving in the depths below his conscious awareness, ponderous and profound as Leviathan exploring the fundaments of the world.

Beside the stone a narrow shore curved into the sedimental base of a high ribbon waterfall which descended from near the rounded summit of Surlej. Leaping from behind the forest pines, the water surged over the alluvial stones in branching channels, then coursed into the lake and expanded across the surface in arcing waves. The steady roar of the falls obscured all other sound, which amplified the signal of the professor's thoughts. Standing alone between the stone and falls, in the shade of the surrounding trees, and the still deeper shade of the mountain on whose slopes they grew, cooled by the chill of the snow-melt water, observing the procession of circular waves, he often realized on this shore a conjoint state of physical tranquility and psychic excitation as in no other place he had ever been.

Three miles north of the stone and falls, after flowing through serene Lake Champfèr, whose little rising wave-crests shimmered and blinked like stars, the Inn twisted through a channel below a stretch of wooded hills, emerged into an open field, then emptied into the pristine waters of Lake St. Moritz. St. Moritz itself, an exclusive resort town recumbent on the slopes below the snow-packed summit of Mt. Corviglia, was a terraced wonderland of elegant homes, posh shops, exclusive hotels, and expensive restaurants. The wealthy, pampered, and privileged citizens of Western Europe flocked to the town seasonally for skiing, hiking, convalescing, or idly relaxing in style. As suitable to the tastes of the aesthete as the contemplative clergyman, St. Moritz attracted a clientele diverse in all but financial resources.

A wandering itinerant writer, as the professor was known to be, will often hear from solicitous acquaintances of cities and towns he absolutely must visit. The weather is milder than anywhere else in Europe! Oh, the wonders the hot-springs will do for your health! The rooms for rent in the local pension are so smartly furnished, and perfectly quiet for writing!

In this way two years earlier the professor had learned of St. Moritz, and as he was feeling unwell at the time, the universal praise of the town's sanatoria prompted him to visit. Unfortunately, his residence there did nothing to improve his health. He recoiled from drinking the malodorous 'miracle cures,' and the other prescribed activities were so pointless and distracting that he soon abandoned them altogether. Yet despite this disappointment, he cherished the area itself, the high heroic mountains framed against Valhalla skies, the modest lake between the town and the spreading acres of woods. If it failed to heal his body, St. Moritz at least enkindled his mind.

The Engadine's high, thin air was especially conducive to the professor's mode of thinking: the curious atmospheric phenomenon by which distant mountains at altitude appear close up, so crisp that one perceives the slightest ridges and crags along the outlines of their peaks, delivered to him the profoundest insights without his having to strain. Walking along the shores of the lake, he regarded the boundless sky reflected on its surface as an image of his own mind; and in those moments he was overwhelmed by joy almost to the point of tears.

In spite of suffering his usual physical agonies, the professor wrote a book that summer in St. Moritz, taking notes while tramping around the lake and the needle-strewn trails in the woods. *The Wanderer and his Shadow*. In a letter to a friend, he wrote of the area that "in this place alone is my true home and breeding ground." He felt, as he put it to another friend, that his personal muses inhabited the place.

Such was the professor's first acquaintance with the Upper Engadine valley. He had intended to lodge in St. Moritz again, and in fact this was his destination when he departed in distress from the spa at Recoaro, from whose famous thermal waters he had received no benefit whatever. But sometime during the long passage beside Lake Como, while observing the luxurious resorts and wealthy summer patrons, he began to stress the expense of lodging in St. Moritz. His anxiety increased with the altitude, and as later he approached Maloja, the uncomfortable ascent through the tortuous pass almost behind him, he shared his concerns with an inquisitive fellow passenger over the din of the rattling carriage. It happened that the man was an Engadine native, and it occurred to him that the reserved professor might well prefer a modest village to the extravagant St. Moritz. He suggested Sils-Maria.

The professor agreed to inspect the town, so the man leaned from the carriage window and directed the driver to turn off at Sils and drop them at the village post-office. After helping the professor collect his bags, and asking the driver to await his return, the stranger led the way to the home of the local grocer, and sometimes mayor, Gian Durisch. By chance he was home, and by chance he had a small but adequate room available to let upstairs in his own house. He explained moreover that since there was a hotel nearby, the professor could take his meals with the Durisch family or, if he preferred, at table with the hotel's summer guests. The fee he requested was less than half the amount the professor had expected to pay in St. Moritz. After inspecting the room, therefore, and surveying Herr Durisch's small but well-stocked grocery, he agreed that the place would suit his needs. He paid out a sum for deposit on the spot, shaking Durisch's hand, and then, grateful to have been relieved of his earlier anxiety, he thanked and bid farewell to the obliging stranger, whom he never saw again, and whose name he never learned.

Herr Durisch assisted his lodger with his luggage, preceding him upstairs, then engaged him in a few minutes of idle conversation. But as it was late in the afternoon, and the professor was exhausted from travel, he soon excused himself, lay down on his bed, and fell asleep without unpacking his bags. He awoke the next morning strained from the previous day's activity, and he feared the onset of one of his fits. Over breakfast he informed the Durisches of his illness, begging pardon in advance for the aggravations attending his condition. But the couple were kind and reassuring. Frau Durisch in particular expressed her concern and assured him of her willingness to tend to him in whatever manner he might require.

That morning he could stomach only tea and bread for a meal, but he experienced a modest upsurge of energy when Frau Durisch spoke of the natural beauties of the area, Lake Sils and Lake Silvaplana in particular, and described the hike through Val Fex to the glacier compacted between the peaks of Mt. Tremoggia and Mt. Fora, beyond whose summits Italy lay. Curious at least to see Lake Sils before returning to his room to rest, the professor left the house with Herr Durisch, who indicated the way to the lake.

Standing there on the porch of Durisch's house, the professor could hardly attend to his landlord's words, so taken was he by the site of Mt. Lagrev gleaming across the way. And when ten minutes later he rounded the line of trees on the far side of the Hotel Alpenrose, and stepped onto the path leading through the meadow to the lake, his breath caught in his throat. He could not move. And as he stood there taking in the stunning view, motionless for a full five minutes, he wondered at the stranger who had intervened so decisively in his life. For it was indeed a life-altering intervention, and even on that first morning the professor knew it well. Grass, flowers, lake, mountains, and sky—the whole of Sils-Maria communicated to him the truth of this, sang it to him as a choir intoning a hymn.

7:30 am – 8:00 am

The natural beauty of Sils-Maria invigorated the professor that first morning of his residence in the town, but he fell ill when the skies clouded over the following afternoon. He did not leave his bed for days; and for much of the next three weeks he was up and down with sickness, never fully recuperated. But now at last he was convalescing, and over the course of the previous eleven days his health had steadily improved. He felt a renewed potency rising in his body, power progressively accumulating, also a brightness enlivening his mood. So here he was again, as on that first glorious morning five weeks earlier, standing on the porch with his back to the door of the Durisch house, admiring luminous Lagrev, which swept up into the sky on the western side of the valley; admiring too, with an excited eye, the colorful meadows spread out before the mountain's forested base.

Stepping from the porch, he balled his hands inside his jacket pockets against the chill rising off the Fedacla, which flowed in front of the Durisches' house on its way from the Fex Valley to Lake Silvaplana. He was comforted by the feel of the bread in the folds of his handkerchief, even more by the presence of his notebook and pencil. As he walked he turned ideas over and back in his mind, formulating thoughts in prose to record on paper. When he mounted the bridge laid over the stream he paused, leaned forward to rest his forearms on the wooden balustrade, facing south with his back to the village. Then, looking down into the rushing water below, he observed the swirling circulations of eddying currents, watched the little flashing white-tips leap from the crests of waves rising over the stones beneath the surface. A multiplicity of individual droplets curled in the air and splashed down again, absorbed into the unity of the whirling stream.

On the trail of a thought regarding the one and the many, the emergence of plurality from original unity and its return thereto, the interblending of opposites and ancient conceptions of Being and Becoming, the professor raised his eyes to track the Fedacla backward against the flow of its current. He traced its course in reverse for a good fifty feet, a broad channel running through the field, then bending left behind a bank of trees which sloped down from the base of Mt. Corvatsch. He knew that from there the gradient increased sharply, that the water fell amid the trees in a tumbling cascade from Val Fex hundreds of feet higher up. He had hiked the ascent beside the falls the previous morning, made the four hour trek to the glacier at the far end of the valley and back.

***

The first twenty minutes of the professor's excursion into Val Fex had exhausted him: leaning on a broken branch for assistance, he struggled up the steep incline beside the plunging water, working up a sweat before emerging from the trees into the open air of the valley, brilliant with rolling hills lushly carpeted green, strewn with flowers of yellow and white and delicate pink, the translucent blue watercourse winding into the distance toward the glacier from which it flowed. Kneeling down beside the stream, he sucked up draughts of water from the cup of his hands, then collapsed on a soft rise under a tree and ate three wedges of an apple Frau

Durisch had sliced and given him at breakfast. He was not long in recovering his breath, but he lingered to take in the scene before him, this high mountain valley more radiant than any natural thing he'd seen before in his life. He thought to himself, "If I were not so confidently in possession of my senses, I could almost believe I had wandered into mother's vision of the afterworld." Then he withdrew his notebook from his pocket and turned to a blank page, on which he wrote a single word, *schön*, 'beautiful,' his penmanship atypically elegant. Then he stood up and silently thanked the tree for its gift of refreshing shade, descended the rise, and stepped onto the path beside the stream, proceeding contrary to the water's course, opposing the current in pursuit of its source.

After an initial incline over a broad knoll, the trail to the glacier was relatively level, curving along beside the river, bending around low rolling hills. To his left the triple peaks of Corvatsch loomed overhead, the summits of snow catching light from the sun just risen from behind the mountain, the exposed granite cliffs below still obscure in the dark. Crooked rows of projecting crags dropped long, narrow shadows into the valley floor. To his right the forested line of south-western hills shone with the morning, the dew-tipped pines radiating light at their crowns and the ends of their branches, their roots entangled and crosshatched with sunlight and shade.

The central run of the valley basked in the full light of the morning sun, mild against the professor's cheek, pleasantly warm across his forehead. He followed the meandering course of the Fedacla, thrilling with every step, exhilarated by the sight of each new bank of flowers, the ethereal hue of the sky. Spinning thoughts revolved around the open field of his mind, rumbling, churning, twisting and tumbling as if driven by high winds. Occasionally he spoke aloud to himself, called out hoots to an eagle screeching from his high perch, plucked flowers and wound them together as chains or tucked them behind his ears.

Thirty minutes into his walk, his attention drawn by a purple blossom just off the path beside him, he happened to see as he glanced down, beneath the ball of his descending foot, a diamond-scaled silver snake crossing into the grass. A shock of adrenaline surged through his limbs, driving him into the air hard off his planted heel with a lopsided hop. Genuinely startled, he was certain the snake would strike his ankle. But as it paid him no attention, merely turned its head to cast an indolent eye in his direction while continuing on its way, he laughed at his alarm and carried on hopping and leaping about, dedicating his dance to the snake as a token of gratitude and friendship.

On the far side of the level stretch of the valley, the trail curved off to the right, diverging from the Fedacla, gradually ascended the ridge at the back of which the massive glacier was packed, then circled back toward the stream atop a high plateau. Passing beside a rough scrub hill, littered with large stones jutting from the ground at wild angles, the trail ran back directly toward the glacier itself. The expansive floor at the glacier's base was littered with rounded rocks through which several channels of run-off water collected to form the Fedacla. Just beyond the point at which the river took definite shape, a small arced wooden bridge spanned the gathering rapids. Two cows stood lazy on the far side, ankle deep in wet grass, taking water.

Stepping onto the bridge, the professor sat down at its apex, dangling his feet over the rushing watercourse. He withdrew the apple wedges from his pocket, tossed one slice each to the cows, then ate the remainder himself, chewing slowly to imitate his bovine acquaintances. For ten minutes these two cows were his most cherished companions on earth, taking their meal in company, comfortable with the silence.

Having settled his stomach, he leaned back on the palms of his hands and swung his legs in the void beneath the bridge. He studied the grey-blue wall of ice before him, traced its every swollen protuberance and jagged fissure, and wondered at the petrified tree protruding perpendicularly from its face. He imagined an enraged titan heaving the shaft into the ice many millennia before.

Beyond the glacier the mountains gradually declined toward the northern plains of Italy, populated from Venice in the east to Turin in the west, Milan an ancient jewel between. The professor recalled his recent sojourn in Recoaro, his longing to abandon the place for the mountains, and the subsequent weeks of misery laid out in bed upstairs in the Durisches' house. His life had run this course for years, intermittently since as a child of thirteen he suffered his first debilitating headache, but worse, much worse, over the past five years. Would he never locate the environment in which he could thrive, identify the diet, physical and spiritual, that would heal him? He was forever on the move in search of health, often believing he had found it. Inevitably he was disappointed. Disappointed and sick. Sick and despairing.

But now was no time to sink into the mire of glum despond. Now the day was brightening, the air thawing warm, the flowers stirring and stretching luxuriantly in the sun. He would be nowhere else on earth at this moment, could imagine no higher life. He felt this in his bones, in his muscles and nerves, as a thrill running over the surface of his skin. Overwhelmed by a sudden rush of joy, he bounded to his feet in celebration of the beauty of Val Fex, and of himself as an observer of that beauty, a participant in it too. He paced back and forth across the bridge, even skipped like a child, leapt and danced, a furious whirling of gestures, sensations, and transitory moods. He shouted to the cows a wild greeting, then recited aloud two verses of a poem he'd lately composed on wisdom as a state infused with folly. The cows stared up at him blankly. The singing sage. The frenzied philosopher.

The professor loitered around the glacier for half an hour. He approached it over the rocks, carefully avoiding the deeper rivulets of run-off water, leaned forward and placed the palms of his hands against the ice, frozen but warm in the sun. Then returning across the stones he mounted a grassy hill to the south of the bridge, sat with his arms embracing his knees, contemplating the scenery from above. The cows had moved to a dry stretch of scrub on the bank just beyond the bridge. They tugged clumps of grass from the ground, masticated lazily, occasionally casting a curious glance at the stranger across the way.

The professor spun around to face the sun and stretch out on his back. He would have the late-morning warmth settle over the entire surface of his body, experience the sunlight gentle on his face, caressing and entrancing him. Behind his eyes he followed ghostly translucent patterns swimming in the darkness, imagined the figures the off-flowing energy of his wild and restless thoughts. The interior of his skull encased an intellectual cosmos, a cavity the size of his fist teeming with an infinity of ideas. The notion made him dizzy. He opened his eyes and sat up, leaning back on his hands.

The arcing sun was nearly overhead now, the temperature rising. The cows were nowhere to be seen. He heard the splashing, frothing water rushing into the valley, the steady swoosh of a murmuring breeze, and nearby, above a waving patch of white flowers, the hum of circulating bees, subtle sounds which deepened the silence of the place.

The atmosphere induced a state of mellow relaxation, and the professor breathed easily, savoring his isolation from the frenetic world of men, their mindless activities and labor. He closed his eyes once again and descended into himself, sank deeper and dissolved into the valley, dispersing as an outflow of energy to merge with the life-force that permeated the soil, the grass, the flowers, water, and air. For a moment he forgot himself, lost himself, or rather lost his *self*, became no-self, was everything and nothing simultaneously.

Thirty minutes later he was making his way back down through the valley, Mt. Lagrev prodigious in the distance wearing a braided cloud for a scarf. The sun burned hot on the back of his neck, and as he walked he occasionally paused to submerge his handkerchief in the Fedacla, wipe his face, then drape the dripping cloth over his head. Proceeding thus beside the surging water, he remarked his progress parallel to the current he'd opposed while advancing earlier toward the glacier from which he now withdrew. No longer contrary motions, he and the river shared the same source and goal. He thought then of the words of Heraclitus: "the road up and the road down are one and the same." He knew that the original Greek was even more obscure, particularly if one refrained from interpolating words not actually present in the text, refrained as well from introducing spaces between the words, which would not have been present in Heraclitus' day: "roadupdownoneandsame." The form of the sentence—a single instance of the word 'road,' the 'up' and the 'down' jammed together—the form no less than the meaning of the words stressed the substance of the thought. Oppositions are constructions of the human mind, which divides original unity into separate substances, individuals with discrete and distinct properties categorized as contrary one to the other. But all such divisions are fabrications, falsifications, fictions. In reality there are neither divisions nor oppositions, only a ceaselessly circulating flow.

Panta rhei: all things flow, precisely like the Fedacla, running off from the glacier through the valley down into Lake Silvaplana below, there to merge with the waters of the Inn on its way to the Danube and Black Sea, later to evaporate, absorbed into sky, later still to coalesce as a drop among drops amassed as a cloud, which falling as rain would begin the round over again. Neither beginning nor end, only…what? Only that which cannot be put into words, including the words 'that which cannot be put into words.' Arriving at a similar insight, Cratylus the ancient Heraclitean refused to speak, would only point or wiggle a finger.

With such thoughts as these flowing through his mind, the professor eventually found himself at the foot of the hill atop which he had rested earlier in the morning. He ascended the rise and sat in the shade of the tree once again, to rest, yes, to relax for a time in silent contemplation of the valley stretched out before him; but more immediately to record a thought in his notebook. On the reverse of the page on which he had written the *schön* while sitting on this very spot upon entering the valley, now before leaving the place he wrote:

> Oh the false opposites! War and peace! Reason and passion! Subject object! Such things do not exist!

The remainder of the day the professor was drained, feeling little beyond a dull fatigue in his limbs. He washed and took a long nap after returning to his room. Later he walked as usual to the far side of Lake Silvaplana, but the mania he'd experienced earlier in Val Fex had long since subsided. His thoughts moved as sluggishly as his heavy legs, and when he returned to his room in the late afternoon, so depleted were his stores of energy he lacked the will to read or write. He could summon only the meager resolve to sit at his table in the dark to rest his eyes. After an hour of this he undressed and lay down to sleep.

***

The morning after this visit to the Fex Valley—which is to say today, *this* morning—the professor awoke disoriented from the dream in which he inhabited the figures of his father and baby brother. And now, not three hours later, he stood on the bridge that spanned the Fedacla, a pause on his way to Lake Sils, leaning against the balustrade, watching the whirling eddies below. Something in the sound of the running water, the hint almost of a melody, and the look of the current curving through the grass and trees, reminded him of the Kleine Saale near Naumburg, the narrow channel diverting water from the Saale River to the grounds of Schulpforta, the boarding school he attended as an adolescent. For a moment in his mind—and in this moment his conscious awareness was confined to the theater of his mind—for a moment he sat at a small desk in a fusty old classroom, transcribing notes from a chalkboard on which his tutor had written a summary of the so-called 'argument from opposites' from Plato's *Phaedo*, which purports to prove the immortality of the soul. All things that have opposites come to be from their opposites. Therefore, as sleep comes from waking and waking from sleep, and as death comes from life, so life must come to be from death. The soul repeatedly cycles through these states, joined with a body in the state known as 'life,' then separated from that body in the state called 'death.' The term 'death' in this instance, then, does not indicate the soul's non-existence, but rather the period during which the soul is separated from the body it previously inhabited, this body having ceased to exist. The soul itself continues on, dissociated from the physical realm until it comes to 'life' again from this separated condition of 'death' by being reborn into a new body. This is one of many arguments through which in the *Phaedo* Plato promotes the Pythagorean doctrine of the transmigration of souls, reincarnation.

According to the obscure teachings of ancient Hellenic mystery cults, echoed by associated philosophical traditions, the soul's original descent into body was punishment for an unspecified primordial sin perpetrated by immaterial beings, the souls themselves, previously uninvolved with the material realm, undefiled by the impulses, lusts, pleasures, and pains of physical bodies. In the *Phaedo* Socrates describes the true philosopher as one who aspires to purify his soul from every bodily distraction and corruption, and thereby at 'death' finally to be liberated from the cycle of rebirth. The purified soul will thus live on eternally in a pure, immaterial realm, perhaps among the gods, but most definitely independent of the muck and mire of physicality.

Standing on the bridge above the Fedacla, the professor recalled the afternoon following this particular lesson, when he stood on a similar bridge above the Kleine Saale, conversing with his schoolmate and friend, Paul Deussen. They had just emerged from class, and, pious Christians that they were, they had their doubts about Plato's reasoning.

"If souls are continually recycled," Deussen wondered aloud, "and if some even are, through purification, eventually withdrawn from the store of recyclable souls, then how is one to explain increasing population numbers? Listen, Fritz: must there not then exist some indefinite number of souls that have not yet entered any physical body, just waiting around for more people to be born? And if so, why have these souls been permitted to avoid for so many millennia the punishment of birth into body long since inflicted on the others?"

Fritz agreed that these were sensible concerns, yet he worried that they had misunderstood the import of Plato's reasoning. "Are we sure he intended us, intended *everyone*—authentic philosophers in particular—to take his reasoning seriously? Socrates says himself that his arguments are dubious and incomplete, and there are hints throughout the text that deeper matters, eccentric ideas, are concealed beneath the surface. My concern," he continued, "is less a matter of the soundness of the arguments than a suspicion regarding our motivations for believing such things. Why, for example, do we cling to our own beliefs about the soul, about God and the afterlife? Because we were taught these dogmata as children; they've been reinforced through years of subtle, and all too often not so subtle, indoctrination; and it's never yet occurred to us to question them. But surely if considered objectively, from the standpoint of unbiased reason, our beliefs must appear no more plausible than Plato's. Or rather: are not Plato's beliefs and our Christian ideals equally *implausible?*"

Thus they reasoned with each other, these two precocious classmates who had knelt together at the altar for their confirmation. Their reverent Christian professions of faith notwithstanding, their encounters with Plato had exposed them both to fascinating pagan spiritual ideas while simultaneously inspiring a critical perspective on spiritual matters in general. In short, the boys had been set adrift on intellectual tides rushing away from the terra firma of religious belief toward the open seas of philosophical doubt. Later they would come to think of themselves as 'free spirits.' Had their mothers known what they were up to, they would have despaired for them as spiritual delinquents bound for eternal confinement in hell.

***

The professor sighed at the thought of his mother fearing for his soul, which she had often expressed in desperate pleadings when he was young, invoking the cherished memory of his father. She was afraid for him still. He loved her for it, but her religious notions no longer had any hold on him. He had overcome the child in himself, the intellectual childhood of man.

Descending the Fex bridge, the professor started down the lane toward Lake Sils, the town-hall on his left, beyond which stood several smaller structures, and at the end of the row, before the meadows to the north of the lake, the Hotel Alpenrose. Just ahead to his right was the village church, drawing near to which he observed a slight, pale figure, whom he took to be the local pastor, standing beside the door affixing a paper notice to a board on the face of the building. Hearing his approaching steps, the man turned and greeted him.

"Ah, hallo, good morning! Yes, good morning to you, sir— Herr Professor! You *are* our visiting professor, no? The Durisches mentioned their boarder to me, and you match their description faithfully. Am I right, then? Am I right? Oh, but pardon me, sir. Pardon me, please. I have forgotten myself. I am Pastor Merian. Good morning!"

"Good to meet you, Pastor," the professor replied with a genial smile. "And, yes, you have as it happens identified me correctly."

As he spoke he observed the bill the pastor had hung on the wall: the words *Ex Nihilo*, written in large Gothic script, headed the page, and beneath this in a smaller and simpler hand was written, "And the Lord said, 'Let there be light.'" The paragraph below this he could not decipher, so poor was his eyesight; but he made out enough of the text to conclude that the notice announced the pastor's Sunday sermon.

"My apologies for not, for not encountering you sooner, Father, but I have been often unwell," and he held out his hand in greeting.

Taking the professor's hand with an embarrassed, "Ah, yes, well, *Pastor*, please," pastor Merian shook it excitedly, with a childlike sort of naive enthusiasm. "In any case, the Durisches tell me you have a particular interest in theology, Herr Professor. Oh, how fine it would be to sit in my garden over tea some warm afternoon, passing the time in conversation, no? It's not often we have such erudite guests resident in our little village. And thanks be to God you're here!"

"Indeed, kind Pastor. Yes. Good conversation is a fine thing indeed," and he glanced again at the pastor's *Ex Nihilo*. "Perhaps I'll see you Sunday morning—if I feel well, that is. I'm afraid this matter is not often up to me, and not always foreseeable. But I shall certainly keep you in mind."

"And I shall remember you in my prayers, Herr Professor. The Durisches have told me of your... of your complications. They've been quite worried for you in fact. But you're looking fit this morning, if I may say so, healthy and fit indeed. Ah, it's splendid, just splendid, and thanks be to God for it! You're walking to the lake, no? An invigorating exercise that, good for the body, even better for the soul—yes, yes—if, of course, one occupies one's mind with devout and moral thoughts. Ah, but who could not think reverently, contemplating the power of our beneficent Creator, when confronted with the majesty of his works in a landscape such as this, on which the evidence of his craftsmanship is everywhere so undeniably stamped? I speak the truth, no? I do, indeed I do, and thanks be to God for it!"

"Well said, Father," the professor replied. "Well said indeed." And with an amiable, "Good day to you, sir," he withdrew from the man and proceeded on his way, turning his head only slightly to nod in reply to the pastor's shouted, "And good day to you, too, Herr Professor! And God's blessings upon you!"

As he walked the professor recalled his student days at Pforta, discussing and debating religion with his friend Deussen. The two young men graduated together, both of them enrolling as students of theology at the University of Bonn. But Fritz soon fully committed to the agnosticism he'd explored during his final year at boarding school. The weekend of his Easter break he scandalized his mother and sister by announcing that he had abandoned his Christian faith, and that he intended, immediately upon returning to university, to transfer from theology to philology, to the study of the languages, literature, and culture of the ancient pre-Christian pagans.

In a letter to his sister written later that year, Fritz elaborated on the details of his intellectual conscience. "Listen, Lama," he concluded, "eventually one grows up, matures intellectually. Anyway *some* men do. For my part, I shall count myself among such courageous men. You must decide for yourself; not even mama can determine your path. And in this field of thought there are two paths, two paths diverging widely, be sure of that. So: If you want only pleasure and a cow's contentment, then believe. If, however, you intend to be an ally of the truth, then you must walk the narrow, uphill path, and *seek it out*!"

8:00 am – 9:00 am

The Professor's youthful apostasy was a genuinely intellectual act, but a strain of adolescent rebellion motivated him as well. He would not have denied the fact himself. His whole life long he intentionally provoked revolutions within himself. Having been the studious intellectual at Pforta, at Bonn for a time he played the libertine. He joined a fraternity called Franconia and indulged in the kind of drunken antics typical of men he would later condemn as benighted adherents of a crude 'beer-materialism.' He did in fact transfer into the department of philology, and as he had been well-trained at Pforta, he performed well enough in his classes. Yet much of his energy he discharged in social activities and other adolescent frivolities. He grew his hair long in the Romantic style, spent lavishly on fashionable items for his wardrobe, money his mother, the pastor's widow, could ill afford. He even rented a piano for his room. He dined out with his fraternity brothers and prowled rural villages on weekends and festival days in search of local celebrations for drinking, dancing, shouting, and drinking still more. He put on weight, his face and belly swelled from the alcohol.

Cajole as he might, Fritz could not convince his friend Deussen finally to abandon his theological studies. "But we philologists study history and the *facts* of things," he would plead. "While you theologians waste your time rummaging around in the dream-world of man, his ignorant nightmares even. Don't you see? You analyze and debate the significance of fantasy-figures and conceptual hallucinations. How can you bear it?!"

Deussen did not disagree. He had admired Fritz as an intellectual mentor since the day they met, and usually he adopted without cavil his academic and cultural judgments. He was eager to follow him in studying philology, too, as he followed him in most everything else. Like Fritz, he had grown out his hair and affected the pose of a young Romantic; he joined the Franconians and participated in their raucous weekend adventures; and as for his theological studies, "Of course you're right," he would say whenever the matter came up, "but my mother has her old heart set on my following my father into the clergy. It's silly, I know. You mustn't doubt that I understand the absurdity of my situation, and that I will find a way to extricate myself in time. I swear."

Fritz and Deussen eventually mastered their self-indulgent passions, but their withdrawal from the dissolute life was as motivated by corporeal concerns as by refined intellectual aspirations. For instance, when Fritz turned up at Deussen's door early one Monday morning, he related a tale that shocked and frightened them both, while dumbfounding them too with hilariously amused disbelief.

According to Fritz's account, he had been out alone in a neighboring town, roaming the streets inebriated. Sometime late in the afternoon, not long before the dinner bells rang, he accompanied a local man who promised to show him the way to a convivial beer-hall. He led him instead to a brothel.

"Oh, Paul, my God," Fritz alternately stammered and laughed as he told the story. "My God, you can imagine my reaction. There was no one of our age or station about, no bouncing band, no dining tables or barmaids. No, the room into which I was directed was dimly lit and swirling with steam and smoke. Velvet drapes and suede divans. Lush but somehow degenerate throw-rugs spread here and there on the unpolished floors. Then a woman entered through a door from the bowels of the place—and, and she greeted me wearing nothing but her undergarments! Actually clad in her underclothes! Then, when several other women appeared similarly attired, or rather likewise disrobed, well, then, as you can imagine, the scales fell from my eyes!"

Deussen grunted, wide-eyed and slack-jawed. He sat back in his seat, gripping the arms of his chair. "Oh, Fritz! Oh, Lord! I can hardly believe what you're telling me now! Are you serious? You *are* serious, yes? All right. And so? So? What on earth did you do?!"

"My God, Paul, what *could* I do? I ask you, really, what could I do? Fortunately," he continued, "I had seen upon entering the, shall we say, the establishment—upon entering the establishment I had seen a piano in the front room. So I'm sure you can guess what I did. I hurried over and sat down at the bench. Anchored myself there. I could not even look at the women. My God, I was actually trembling! Well, in any case, I did the only thing I knew to do. I gathered myself as best I could. I played. I improvised—*pianissimo*, you understand, to calm my nerves and, I hoped, to dampen the, the ladies' passions."

"Ha! But Fritz, my God, I really can't believe this!" Leaning in now, forearms on his knees. "But, yes, sorry. Go on, please do go on."

"Well, that's about the end of it, really. At one point I glanced up from the keyboard. Some of the women had left the room. Others were staring at me, in mockery or disbelief or admiration I couldn't begin to tell. Suddenly it occurred to me—foolishly, I know, but I was hardly in my right mind, you understand—the dreadful thought assailed me that my playing might actually produce an effect contrary to that intended, that rather than check their spirits the music might, ah, what does one say?, that it might *stoke the fires of their lust*. Ha!"

Deussen laughed too, sitting back in his chair and slapping his thighs.

"Oh, God," Fritz caught his breath and continued, "and with this image in my mind I quite literally leapt up and pushed the bench behind me in a single frantic motion of my legs. On my way passing through the room I attempted—oh, how pitifully I tried!—I attempted a sophisticated bow, of pardon and leave-taking combined, but I know I looked a fool. And then out the door and down the street. I had to pause for several minutes in an alley on my way out of town—I felt I would vomit, literally disgorge my afternoon's lunch and the pints of beer sloshing around on top of it!"

The boys never forgot this incident. Often when they were in company together, when spirits were high and the cross-talk loud, Deussen would call out to his friend, "Ho there, Fritz, play us a tune at the piano, *pianissimo*, you know, to *stoke our fires*!" The remark made sense to no one, but it never failed to induce fits of laugher in the two old friends.

As humiliating to Fritz as his abortive evening with the prostitutes admittedly was, it was a different variety of awkward encounter that finally redirected him from his errant ways back to the path of his studious inclinations. On a weekend afternoon carousing with the Franconians in the Bonn city center, he provoked a drunken quarrel with a member of another fraternity. The subject of their disagreement was vague; probably neither understood the other's point. The driving force behind the affair was less the substance of the dispute than the adolescent impulse to act the part of the brash young man, intensified by blind inebriation. In a moment of confused silence following a stammering collapse of the argument, Fritz blurted out a challenge: "Perhaps, then, we should settle this matter as gentlemen, with sabers drawn." His rival agreed, from embarrassment before his peers if not from a noble sense of duty or courage, and their drunken fellows standing round cheered and toasted the fun.

When Deussen learned of the impending duel, and his pleadings failed to dissuade Fritz from participating, he insisted on joining him as his second. Therefore on the weekend after the original quarrel, on a Sunday afternoon, the two friends rode together in a carriage out of town, trailed by their Franconian brothers, some of them already well on their way to a state of stumbling drunkenness. Inside an old abandoned barn, an isolated structure standing in a field known as the Wayland, the members of the two fraternities formed a circle around the combatants. The two young men shook hands, nervous but trying to affect an air of muscular nonchalance, then they took their swords from their seconds.

"Fritz," Deussen whispered to his friend upon relinquishing the weapon, "keep in mind this is only a game. No one is to be hurt here. Especially not you!"

Fritz replied with a nod of the head, his eyes flashing panic and reckless resolve. Then, after formally bowing and crossing swords, the two young men circled each other, feinting and withdrawing to the cheers and imprecations of the crowd.

Deussen balled his fists in his overcoat pockets, chewed his lip and said a prayer for his friend. Less afraid for Fritz's life than anxious and exasperated at his recklessness, he kept silent and waited impatiently for the contest to conclude. He did not have long to wait. In the fit of a flurry of undisciplined thrusts and evasions, Fritz lunged forward, slashing wildly, and drew blood from above his opponent's left eye. The other retreating stretched out his arm, locked at the elbow, with the result that as Fritz stepped toward him he ran into his saber's sharp tip. Blood poured from the bridge of his nose.

With blood drawn on both sides, and each of the duelists shaken, the crowd cheered and rushed the young men, gathered around them leaping and laughing and recounting the action with excited hyperbole. Amid the confusion the rivals clasped hands and formally pronounced the matter resolved.

Deussen fought his way through the mob to his friend, pressed a handkerchief against his nose and drove him home. "Thank God that's over," he groaned repeatedly, to which Fritz eventually replied, "Thank Ares, yes, and Hebe too!" Then they laughed and agreed to speak no more of the matter except as a childish prank of youth, evidence of immaturity indulged and overcome.

***

The professor proceeded down the lane away from the village chapel, fingering the scar on the bridge of his nose, his exchange with the pastor forgotten among these memories of his youth. The lascivious red shades of the brothel; nausea in the alley; gleaming swords and the din of raucous spectators; blood running warm down his nose.

As he approached the Hotel Alpenrose, still massaging his scar, he marked a modest increase in his heart rate, felt a warmth expanding across his face, a tingling on the surface of his cheeks. He was blushing, embarrassed by these memories of his immaturity. How silly he had been, how imprudent and rash! He had wasted the better part of a year on distractions and childish indulgences! Fool!

But welling up from beneath this torrent of self-condemnation, a counter train of thought appeared. "Why after all should I reject my youth and convict my past? Shall I place my own life on the scales of value and find it wanting? What good could possibly come from this? Was I a fool? So be it! Mustn't one be a fool at times, especially the man on his way to wisdom—for is not the wise man also a fool? And as my illness presently affects me, influences and molds me, has not my past shaped me too, contributed to my being the man I am today? Shall I then condemn who I am? Shall I condemn my minor transgressions, my occasional vices, my illness and my suffering, and thereby condemn *myself*? This is no way to overcome suffering, to rise above it into a flourishing health. No, he who convicts himself compounds his suffering, succumbs to his pain, is bested by his worst self. He draws the gloomy conclusions of his illness and thereby makes himself *more sick*, which renders him in turn more prone to sickness. So if I would be healthy, vigorous in body and spirit alike, I must strive to *affirm* my past, my present and future too. For what *am* I but my past, present, and future? And what are my vices and my illness but stimulants to my particular virtues and higher health?"

Thus the professor spoke to his heart as he approached Lake Sils. And he had it in mind to record these insights in his notebook when he rounded the turn beyond the Alpenrose and was, as usual, overwhelmed by the natural beauty before him. The meadows, the lake, the mountains and sky rushed forward to occupy every fold of his brain, displacing every other thought; a cool, distracting wind blew through his bones; the slanting rays of morning light entranced him; the dancing colors of the awakening flowers delighted him; the intermittent cawing of crows on the wing echoed enchantingly through his mind; and the mystic glow infusing the scene induced in him a state akin to rapture. He froze on the spot, stood engrossed for several seconds passing slow, creeping as if time would stop. Then he shook himself and proceeded along a dusty path that angled through the meadow toward a low stone wall. There he sat down and folded his hands between his knees, concentrated to regulate his respiration—inhale, relax; exhale, relax—and focused his attention on the view.

Casting his eyes across the meadow and beyond the lake, the professor traced the peaked outlines of mountain ridges against the sky. Inclined planes descending to the east and west of the pass behind Maloja, the great cloudless negative space of sky between the sloping bases. The scene moved him every time he looked on it, morning, afternoon, or evening; he loved it even with clouds, especially the small stray cumulus cloud, drifting aimless, wispy around the edges, bearing no rain. But a cloudless unobstructed blue was best. This morning the sky was a crystalline pure infinity, and the mirroring waters of the lake, reflecting and redirecting the light, diffused the sky's azure hue throughout the shimmering atmosphere.

Ex Nihilo! He thought he'd heard the words spoken aloud. He turned to look over his shoulder, expecting to find pastor Merian standing behind him. But he was alone, a solitary point of consciousness surrounded by meadow, mountains, and sky.

Ex Nihilo! He imagined the pastor at work inside his church, recollecting their earlier exchange, relishing the mini-sermon he'd delivered to the pious professor. This landscape as the handy-work of an omnipotent craftsman deity. Ha!

Ex Nihilo! He dismissed the idea with a wave of his hand.

The professor had not believed in a beginning of time for years. The thought of a pre-time un-filled with non-being suddenly transformed by a miraculous '*Fiat lux*!' into a plenum of temporality and being—this thought struck him as ridiculous. He had learned from the Greeks to scorn the idea of creation from nothing as empty verbiage. *Ex nihilo nihil fit*! At most one might admit the possibility of construction from previously existing materials, as Plato in the *Timaeus* depicts the Demiurge fashioning the world from eternally existing triangles. Then there were those like the Stoics, some of the Pythagoreans, and possibly even Heraclitus, who insisted that time cyclically recurs in great tides of cosmic intervals, neither beginning nor ending nor always unfolding on the way to ever new beings and novel states, but eternally returning to the same beings and identical states.

The Christian view of creation had displaced every earlier Greek idea with its fantasies of a temporal progression enclosed at one term by a void, a void supposedly empty but occupied in fact by an infinite being somehow acting with no time in which to act, an intentional being who infuses temporal succession with a *telos*, an aim, a goal, and therefore by implication with a narrative plot-line progressing from beginning to end, each individual playing its role in a preconceived plan, every event assigned a specific meaning and purpose. This view had been taught for so long, promulgated with the sanction of authority, and more often than not with the threat of a merciless force unleashed against unbelievers, that eventually it became the standard view, rarely questioned, certainly never publically.

Recently, however, after centuries of an incremental waning of the Church's influence, the Christian conception of time had come under fire, first in the philosophy of Immanuel Kant, later in the form in which the professor first encountered it, namely, in the work of Arthur Schopenhauer. Schopenhauer had taught him to think of time as a form of human intuition, which is to say as an *a priori* category of experience, an aperture of the mind, as it were, through which every sensation of the world must pass on its way into human consciousness, and by which perceptions are imbued with temporal qualities their objects do not possess in and for themselves. Humans cannot help but perceive events *in time*, not because time is real in itself, but rather because the human mind necessarily imposes temporality on experience. It is therefore quite impossible to conceive of either a beginning or an end of time. Wherever the human mind wanders, in experience, thought, or imagination, time necessarily attends it.

The professor tried, as he sometimes did, to recall Kant's specific terminology, his every minute conceptual distinction, but as usual he dismissed the endeavor as a pointless indulgence in pedantry. Schopenhauer's system had the virtue of completeness combined with simplicity and clarity. Besides, what mattered was the general insight into the endlessness of time, which was maintained as well by many contemporary physicists and cosmologists, whose thoughts on the matter were these days dearer to him even than Schopenhauer's.

Reviewing this history while contemplating the mountains in the distance, it occurred to the professor that the thesis of an infinite extent of time is neutral between the conception of an endlessly linear temporal succession and the idea of time's eternal recurrence. Why, then, he wondered, why had Kant and Schopenhauer adopted so readily, and so unquestioningly, the notion of a linearly progressive time?

"Christianity, of course!" he thought. "Of course, and as usual!"

With Kant this was no surprise. Kant was an underhanded Christian from the start. Schopenhauer was both more honest and more cautious; but even he, it seemed, had failed to transcend his heritage. His conception of time was as influenced by the Christian intellectual tradition as Christian assumptions had infected and perverted his pessimism. Even Plato, after all, had possessed the power and independence of mind to conceive of the so-called 'Great Year,' the periodic cycling of the heavenly bodies around the earth until, at the completion of the perfect number of revolutions, they return to their original positions relative to one another. True, he had omitted to explain the consequences of this event, but one could imagine...

"But, ah, that old Schopenhauer," the professor interrupted himself. "What a disappointment he was after all! A frank and unflinching pessimist, but weak, alas, a pessimist from weakness. My 'educator,' no doubt. But, in the end, a rung on the ladder of my self-overcoming. Like everything else. Like every experience, every emotion, every thought, and, indeed, like everyone—every person—else!"

And with this thought he recalled his old friend Deussen, who had been often on his mind of late. Ten years had passed since last they'd seen each other, in 1871, when Deussen came to Basel for a visit. In the autumn of that year, on a Monday night near the end of a cold October, the professor returned to his rooms from dining out with a colleague to find his friend on the steps outside his apartment, an overnight bag in his hands. What a delight it was to see him! They had not been together since Fritz transferred from Bonn to the university in Leipzig. Deussen had stayed behind in Bonn, still obedient to his mother's wishes, still entangled in the constricting net of his theological studies. When they parted there were tears, and maudlin oaths of friendship, but their studies and, later, their respective careers had intervened. They maintained contact through the post, but the intimacy of their youth was gone. Then they had their fun reminiscing and laughing through the night in Basel, old friends at last in company again. But that was it. The day was done, and Deussen had to leave.

***

Sitting in the morning light of Sils, the sun obscured by a stray cloud of wistfulness drifting through his mind, its shadow lingering over his heart, the professor recalled Schopenhauer's words, "Time is that which always makes fools of us, and we never see through its little game." "Indeed!" he reflected. "What fools we are indeed. Every one of us. Loving only to lose. Living only to die. Ah, friend Deussen! How I sometimes miss our youth, and long to live it again."

These days the professor lived his life more or less in isolation, shuttling between the cities and towns of Northern Italy and Switzerland, rarely visiting friends or family, seldom encountering a familiar face. He would see Paul Deussen only one more time in his sane life, in the summer of 1887, six years almost to the day of his sitting on this wall, in this meadow, remembering his youth. Recently married, Deussen brought his wife to the Engadine to meet the retired professor, the free-spirited hermit who styled himself 'the cave-bear of Sils-Maria.' What a shock, that visit. Deussen later recalled that his old friend was drained of his former youthful vigor. He was pallid and weak; he shuffled unsteadily when he walked; and his words came slowly, often in a stammering confusion. The professor made light of his condition, blaming it on the weather, the troops of rainclouds darkening his beloved sky. But when Deussen visited his old friend's room upstairs in the back of the Durisch house, he could only conclude that his disorder was worse than the matter of a day. The place was a mess: the bed unmade; a broken dish on the bedside table; dead flowers drooping in a vase; papers strewn about, on the table, on the bed, crumpled or torn on the floor. The sweet smell of medicine and narcotics lingered in the air, rising off a tray on the bureau littered with overturned phials and spilled pills.

Deussen met his childhood friend only one other time after that, in celebration of his fiftieth birthday, six years after his annihilating mental collapse. He brought as a gift a large bouquet of flowers, presented it to him personally, but the professor did not recognize him. When prompted he spoke of Pforta, and of "friend Deussen" too; but he did not associate the man before him with the fragments of scrambled memories limping through his disjointed mind.

Deussen blamed his friend's breakdown on his irregular life, his hermetic seclusion, his irresponsible practice of self-medication, and the frenzied speed with which from youth he stormed headlong into every alleyway of thought, heedless of his own well-being. He had first known Fritz as a restive youth, an aspiring intellectual infused with the spirit of an untamed colt. From a distance he watched him mature into a brilliant thinker and author—into, in a word, a philosopher. But in later years he often wondered whether the man had ever really overcome his adolescent recklessness. And what did it suggest, he asked himself, what did it indicate, that his old friend's pursuit of wisdom had led him finally into a labyrinth at the center of which there lurked in the shadows, salivating on its haunches, the furious, the ungovernable, the hideous Minotaur of madness?

9:00 am – 10:00 am

The professor stood up from the low stone wall and made his way through the meadow toward Chastè, the larches on its eastern flank fully bathed in light. A shade of sadness troubled a nook of his heart, but as he moved his body came to life; his muscles and nerves, lungs and limbs, quickened, his stride slow but powerful, his body erect. With every step his mood began to lift. He sensed this and smiled at his resilience.

Stepping onto the path that ran along the peninsula's shore before curving toward the interior, he put his distracted year at Bonn out of mind and turned to thinking instead of Leipzig, the town in which his life at last began to take a definite shape. He had transferred there to study with Professor Friedrich Ritschl, who had himself left Bonn to join the Leipzig department of philology. In addition to this changing of schools, Fritz was determined to change himself, to master his recalcitrant will, to finally put behind himself the undisciplined, unserious, superficial life he'd lived in Bonn. He rented a room from a local bookseller and set himself up as a young scholar in training. He would live ascetically; he would become a serious man, studious and self-disciplined. He had just turned twenty-one.

A scholar he became indeed, the brightest star in the firmament of his generation of students. He studied the archaic lyric poets and Pre-Platonic philosophers, publishing the prodigious fruits of his research in scholarly and literary journals. He co-founded the Philological Society, which attracted as members the most dedicated of his university peers. He applied himself industriously to his many academic endeavors. Yet as busy as he was, he still found time to indulge his passions for music, poetry, and literature. Professor Ritschl was impressed. He'd never before encountered such a brilliant young phenomenon. He encouraged his talented student, his favorite, befriended him too; and he praised and promoted his work at every opportunity, public and private.

Fritz's remarkable growth as a scholar was not his most significant experience in Leipzig. More important still, more fateful, the event which effected a deeper and more enduring change in his life, befell him quite by accident. Rummaging around in his landlord's bookshop late one afternoon, he happened upon a volume of Arthur Schopenhauer's magnum opus, *The World as Will and Representation*. Impressed by what he read, the style as well as the substance, he carried the book home and studied it closely. 'Closely' soon progressed to *enthusiastically*, then to *passionately*, perhaps even *obsessively*. Quite apart from Schopenhauer's specific philosophical ideas, young Fritz was struck by the man's personality, which manifested in every line of his text, in every delicious turn of phrase, one might even say in every word. Schopenhauer was no university drone, churning out work in support of the state, to defend religion, or to further his own professional career. He was an independent thinker and writer, working within the Kantian tradition while struggling against the worst of its vices, its verbal obscurantism, conceptual profligacy, pedantic insipidity. Schopenhauer was, in short, a rare amalgamation of erudite intellectual and bold iconoclast. To Fritz the mixture was seductive as a witches' brew. Schopenhauer excited the twin dominant aspects of his personality, his youthful rebelliousness and his mature self-disciplined gravity, an internal opposition he never resolved, but which in time he learned to manage. More, he trained himself to harness it, to exploit and to grow from it, to channel the energy thrown off by every inner conflict into his goal of personal expansion and ascension.

***

Sitting now on his usual bench on the southern rise of Chastè, the professor removed Frau Durisch's bread from his jacket pocket, released it from the folds of his handkerchief, and tore a thick corner from the whole. He broke the piece in half, tossed one part into the water and the other behind him into the trees. For the gods and for the animals. Then spreading his handkerchief across his lap, he broke small segments from the bread and consumed them one by one. As he ate he gazed into the water below, which reflected the sky above. Then he followed the ridge-line of the mountains to the east, which running south from Sils-Maria declined behind Maloja, then rose again as a line of ridges to the west running north back toward town. "All things that have opposites come to be from their opposites." Once again he recalled this line from Plato's *Phaedo*, which stirred another memory of the work. Near the beginning of the dialogue Socrates likens the opposites of pleasure and pain to a pair of men joined at the crowns of their heads. Whenever one approaches, the other is sure to follow. The professor imagined such a man, a crooked thing, a hooped circle, a mirror turned toward itself.

"Oh, that blasted Plato," he spoke the words aloud. Then, silently, "So close to Heraclitus in so many ways. Yet in the end so distant. So distant and so wrong. Becoming *and* Being. As if that little 'and' were inconsequential, harmless even. Would that it were! Here we have a pseudo-opposition so fantastical, so thoroughly illegitimate, that it's no use trying to resolve it by reducing its two terms to underlying unity, for one of the terms is non-existent, a fiction. *Being*, ha! A concept as empty as *God*, and as pernicious!"

These thoughts as he rehearsed them manifested and dissolved in his mind, and the quanta of psychic energy deposited in their wake gradually collected and took shape as a mood, as an image, and finally as a memory in the figure of a man. Erwin Rohde, whom Fritz met soon after moving to Leipzig, was a fellow philologist and, even better, an enthusiastic disciple of Schopenhauer. The two young men bonded immediately, and throughout their time in school they were rarely apart. Professor Ritschl called them 'the Dioscuri,' the twins, Castor and Pollux.

The original Castor and Pollux, mythological heroes, were hatched from an egg, Pollux having been fathered by Zeus in the form of a swan, Castor by Tyndareus, a human whose mortality Castor inherited. When Castor died, the immortal Pollux persuaded Zeus to permit him and his brother to take turns living. Therefore the twins cycle daily from life to death, from death to life.

"All things from their opposites," the professor mused. "And into their opposites they return. A never-ending cycle." He thought then of the cycle of his own life, his own existential and psychic oppositions. In a way, his relationship with Rohde expressed externally his personal internal contradictions. As he was in his spirit both a philosopher and a scholar, so in public Rohde played the diligent scholar to his free-spirited philosopher. It had always been this way with him, though rarely as evidently as now, now that he had retired from the university. His present way of living was unmistakably opposed to his former life as a scholar, and to the present lives of his few remaining academic friends. He went his own way, unapologetically, a habit he'd indulged since childhood. This independent spirit alienated him from many a friend over the years, and more recently even from his family. But the more isolated he was from the common way of men, and despite the pangs of loneliness and longing which often overwhelmed him, the firmer grew his conviction that his divergent path through life must lead to his authentic self and task. His was an uncommon goal, no doubt, exceptional, singular, a goal from which most other men would shrink if they could see it. But they could not see it. It was his goal, his alone, and he would do whatever it took to achieve it, regardless of the eccentricities of life the endeavor imposed on him.

Fritz's idiosyncratic dual nature erupted again during his student years in Leipzig, at a time when he was determined to restrict his activities to the narrow task of training for the life of a scholar, and this even though he managed to impose a severe self-discipline on himself, an asceticism encouraged by his reading of Schopenhauer. Schopenhauer taught that the essence of life is will, specifically the Will to Live. But this will itself is blind, aimless, a ceaseless, insatiable striving. As a consequence of the will's insatiability, suffering is inherent in human life: we suffer the lack of the object of our willing, and if we ever happen to attain it, we soon become bored and must will a new object, from whose lack we suffer all over again. The only way to eliminate suffering, then, is to suppress our willing nature; but since this nature is of our essence, to suppress it we must deny our will to live—not through suicide, which Schopenhauer conceived as an act expressing a frustrated will to live, quite the opposite of the denial of this will; but rather through renunciation, abstinence, a western variety of the Buddhists' purging of desire.

This doctrine of denial suited Fritz's needs as a student. Shunning all diverting and pointless indulgences, he dedicated his time and energy to reading and writing. Rohde adopted the practice too. The pair were at the center of a lay monastic brotherhood of student-scholars, around which other committed students gathered; but none was so dedicated, none went to such extremes of personal austerity, as the Dioscuri. They were almost religious in their fervor. They even had an icon, a portrait of the master, Schopenhauer himself, which Rohde had given to his friend as a gift. "Take this," he said when handing over the small framed picture, wrapped lightly in colored tissue paper. "Take this, and look on the sublime countenance whenever your determination flags. Behold the peace that's possible through right-living, and thereby reinforce your own resolve."

Fritz eagerly unwrapped the gift, beaming, for he could see the portrait through the gauze. "Oh, thank you, friend," he replied. "Thank you very much indeed! We'll set this in a place of honor in my front room. Whenever we meet we'll have this paragon before us. And with the master's help, and our own mutual assistance, we shall, to adapt Pindar, become who we are meant to be."

In the course of such conversations, the young men often expressed their personal dreams and scholarly aspirations. "I hope one day to write the history of the development of the notion of the immortal soul," Rohde would say, his eyes distant, his voice low, as if he were lost in a daydream. Then, high-pitched with excitement, "Since no such soul exists, the story of the Greeks' coming to believe in it—falling for it, I might say—can't help but be enlightening. It might also be liberating, for to watch a thing come to be is to learn at least that it's contingent—and that which has come to be must one day cease to be in turn."

To speculations such as this Fritz would reply, "Indeed! A remarkable idea, that! As for me, I shall labor to liberate the Pre-Platonics' radical insights from centuries of dry scholarly encrustations. And I should also like to reveal something of their personalities. For if the idea of an immortal soul attains its fullest expression in the Platonic tradition, then knowledge of thinkers prior to Plato and Socrates must provide access to an authentically tragic thought-world, ancestor to our Schopenhauer's philosophy, which informed men's minds before they were infected by the shallow optimism of Plato and his spiritual descendants, the Christians."

And when, inevitably, the conversation turned to personal matters, Rohde would advise his friend to take a young wife, "someone to look after your wayward heart. For, you know, books and a portrait, and even the force of a determined will, require now and then a living presence for encouragement, succor, and support. We both know your tendency to wander, to play the Dionysian, untamable in your frenzy. Ha! A wife, a comfortable academic post, and perhaps a child, too—God,

Fritz, really, I can hardly imagine it—you with a child!—but, anyway, yes, a steady solid life is just the thing for you."

His imagination overheated from the fervor of their talk, Fritz would yield to his friend's judgment, sometimes even agree enthusiastically. "Yes," he would say, "and you, too. You will settle down for sure. And we'll find you a post near to me, in a readily accessible university town. We'll meet to toast the *daimones* together, securing the blessings of the ancestral spirits."

But Fritz could never reconcile himself to settling for long into a secure routine. The force of his drives running counter to his academic aspirations was all too powerful. Therefore, as dedicated as he was to his studies and research, he relished the radical alteration of his circumstances when he was called up to serve in a Prussian regiment during an outbreak of hostilities with Austria. He was away from school for a year, and for the first six months of his service he was made to drill for hours every day, learning to deploy, load, and fire heavy artillery, and training to ride a warhorse. The military life was more brutal than he'd anticipated, hard on his mind and body alike; and as he reported to Rohde in his letters, he was often moved to appeal for assistance to Schopenhauer's shade, invoking the ghost through his portrait. Yet, as exhausting as this new routine undeniably was, he enjoyed it, or anyway he appreciated it, for he regarded the experience as an opportunity to develop yet another side of his personality, to add a novel perspective to his armamentarium of intellectual weaponry, which is how he'd come to think of his time among the Franconians too. At Bonn he experienced adolescent debauchery from the inside. Through his military training he was gaining insight into man's physicality and violent nature, the will to cruelty and the lust for power.

Fritz's study of Schopenhauer—and, more specifically, his reading *about* Schopenhauer, the man himself as a living agent—had reinforced his own assessment regarding the value of developing oneself in a multiplicity of directions, not just as a scholar but as a *whole man*—as a scholar, yes, but also as a seeker and a wanderer, a terrestrial explorer and intellectual adventurer, a collector and connoisseur of experiences, a tempter and attempter, a prankster, a fool, an artist, a poet, a thinker and a dreamer, a man of science and a lover of wisdom.

Rohde never understood this about his friend, never liked it, his conflicting drives, his will to celebrate, even to incite, the conflict. The disposition struck him as dangerous, as a threat to one's future. And he was right, too—if, that is, one has in mind a bourgeois future, a conscientious life as a family man and docile academic. But despite his smiling consent whenever Rohde encouraged him to settle into the routine of a conventional life, Fritz understood that in fact he intended no such life for himself. He finally admitted this to his heart in Leipzig, precisely when he appeared to everyone—and to Rohde in particular—to be advancing single-mindedly toward just this goal.

***

"No, I never intended such a life for myself," the professor reflected, shaking the breadcrumbs from his handkerchief. "Alas, my friends have never understood my double-, my triple-, my multiple-mindedness. Not one among the lot of them. But, oh, friend Rohde! 'γένοι' οἶος ἐσσὶ': was not this our motto? 'Become who you are!' Did we not agree on this above all else? Yet it seems that you disliked the man I would become. You wanted me to stay put, to stagnate, simply to *be*. Ah, and here again we return to the source of so many misunderstandings: Plato and his Being. Son of the Eleatics' One. Father of the Christians' God. What a disaster these deceptions have been, for individual lives as well as for entire cultures! But must I remain forever alone in comprehending these things? So it seems. Therefore I must learn to live with this, my high-mountain solitude and aloneness, my eternally unpartnered untimeliness. But must I learn even to *love* it? Yes, I suppose I must. Even love. Even this. This and everything else, too. For, after all, I do hope one day to be only a Yes-sayer."

As close as they once were, Fritz and Rohde, the Dioscuri, had drifted apart in recent years, particularly after Rohde married; and the physical distance between them exacerbated preexisting tendencies to misunderstanding. They stayed in touch by letters, and the professor sent his old friend copies of his books as they appeared; but more and more their erstwhile harmony had dissolved into a subtle but undeniable discord. In his letters Rohde was distant. He sometimes affected the tone of the distracted family man, too busy to attend to the emotional vicissitudes of one so mercurial as his tempestuous friend. This tone became even more prominent after the birth of Rohde's son. He was a father now; he could not look after his child and a grown man too. Hadn't his friend played "the Dionysian solitary" long enough by now? Should he not finally join "the world of responsible men and women, of conventional roles and relationships"? It would do him good. As if he hadn't learned by now to recognize his own good!

As for the professor's books, his most recent works, of which he was especially proud, Rohde's assessments were polite but reserved. He seemed sincerely to appreciate the professor's prose style, and some of his ideas too. But on the whole he was dismissive, and at times the professor detected an undercurrent of hostility. He had heard through an acquaintance, who had heard from someone else, that in conversation with a common friend Rohde had spoken contemptuously of his latest publication, *Daybreak*. He did not push for details, nor even ask the identity of the friend, from embarrassment or pride he could not himself say. But he was wounded in his heart. Disagreement he could take, even relish. As he had written in more than one letter over the years: "What, after all, is an intellectual dispute between friends—what but a stimulus to deeper and richer friendship? Ah, old friend, let us disagree and be glad of it!" But this hostility, this disdain? This he could not comprehend. Were Castor and Pollux not eternal allies, even unto death, even after death? How then could his own twin finally turn against him, apparently even attempt to undermine his authority and reputation? As capacious and pliable as his mind was, he could not stretch it to fit this image of his friend. The exertion caused him no end of grief. After reading the note that informed him of Rohde's "contempt," he laid it aside and wept.

The professor looked across Lake Sils toward Maloja. The mountains shone in the sun, which by now had fully risen over

Corvatsch. Not a cloud in the sky. Yet the professor was overshadowed, and not only by the larch and pine trees surrounding him. He was thinking of a letter he'd received from Rohde earlier in the year, to which he had yet to respond. He was by nature a conscientious correspondent, but this letter had rattled him. He had written two replies immediately after reading it, but he discarded them both. Then he folded the letter, slipped it between the pages of the book he was reading at the time, and let it sit. He did not forget it—to the contrary, he tried but could not put it out of his mind. Accompanying the letter was a photograph of Rohde sitting with his wife and child, and this photograph, even more than the melancholy mood of the letter itself, disturbed him. He regarded the portrait as a reverse image of himself, for it represented everything he was not and would never be. Tranquility, contentment, and the steady peace of familial love glowed as an aura around the happy faces. The stark opposition to his own situation upset him even though he understood that he would never change places with his friend. He did not want peace and contentment, rather even deeper solitude, more intense suffering. For hardship breeds strength, tenses the will, and reveals to a man his one thousand and one ingenious means of mastering his pain. To bear up and conquer hardship—physical, emotional, and psychological hardship—is to train oneself in self-overcoming. And continual self-overcoming, constant transcendence of present conditions into superior future states—he had adopted this ceaseless activity of striving as his personal intellectual and existential practice. He had recently taken to calling it his "cheerful scientific method."

Still, the professor's embrace of suffering as a stimulus to ascent was no proof against the natural consequences of pain. He was human after all. He ached from loneliness and wept from grief like everyone else. In fact, he often suspected that he suffered more profoundly than his fellows, that it was precisely the shallowness of their suffering that enabled them to endure it with such paltry medicines as work and family. Rohde was shallow in this way, apparently, though once he had seemed to contain depths. And the professor could not avoid it: occasionally in moments of depressed weakness, he longed to be shallow too.

He removed his notebook and pencil from his jacket pocket, and turning the notebook over, he opened it to a page near the back and wrote:

Friend Rohde,

Do forgive my tardiness in replying. And, please, accept my gratitude for the photograph you sent. What a charming family you are! The very paradigm of bliss! How happy I am for you!

I must admit, however, that I read behind your eyes, and between the words of your kind note, a wistful sentiment of friendship fled. It is as if you would say to me, 'What friends we once were, what happy companions! And now? Now we seem to live in different worlds!'

Alas, old friend, this is how it is with me these days. Everyone I meet is cordial, to be sure, irreproachably polite. But even my oldest friends speak to me now in a single voice, whether in person or in writing: 'Alas, dear,' they say, 'we must leave you now. It was good to see you, really so very fine to see you again. But now, old friend, now you are *all alone.*'

He read the note over and decided that soon—today or tomorrow—he really must finally write to Rohde and be done with it. Though he had neglected the chore for months, he sensed its burden whenever he encountered the book in which he had enclosed the letter. He returned his notebook and pencil into his pocket, and with a parting glance at the water below, he stood up to leave.

But in fact he did not stand up. *Could* not stand up. And it dawned on him with the exertions of a moment that he was altogether unable to move. Even his thinking was sluggish. It was as if he were dreaming. Or rather remembering. Or, no, he thought, he seemed trapped somehow in a state between the two. One knows when one is remembering, for one experiences the memory as a mental event inside one's head. But when dreaming one experiences one's physical head, and indeed one's whole self, inside the dream. The professor's experience manifested in the form of a memory, but a memory he inhabited, a memory through which, or in which, he was living. A memory, moreover, which had only a hint of past-ness about it. Rather, a note of futurity permeated his experience: it felt less a recollection than a *pre*-collection. A memory of the future…

Now there was no Lake Sils before him, no Chastè, no mountains or sky. Sils-Maria itself was missing. The professor was sitting up in bed, two pillows behind his back. His arms hung loose over cotton sheets bunched up on his lap. He was weak, enfeebled. He could feel the hair on his head, thick and greasy as if it had not been washed for weeks. His moustache was tangled and overgrown; thick stray hairs itched his chin. He faced a large window inside an unfamiliar room. The air around was close and musty.

Where am I?

He heard noises nearby but could not turn his head to discover their source. He was waiting, only waiting, as if waiting was all he had ever done. Then he went blank, his field of vision dark, only a low droning hum inside his skull. Black static.

Then a radiance of light penetrated the darkness, and opening his eyes he saw his sister's face before him, close, and moving closer. She was much older than he was now.

Lama, what has…

But he could not form the words. He felt her hand run through his hair, her breath against his ear.

"Brother, do you hear me? I'm afraid I have sad news for you, love. Erwin Rohde—you remember your old friend Rohde, yes? I hate to have to tell you, dear, but Rohde is dead."

He heard the words distinctly, but the sound confused him. Rohde dead? The expression connected with nothing on the surface of his awareness, slid frictionless across the ice of his frozen consciousness. But the sentiment resonated through his depths, roiled the darker, liquid layers of his mind.

"Rohde is dead."

He sensed the fathoms within him, layer upon layer weighing him down, felt ponderous waves rolling beneath the ice, slowly, powerful, spreading out in grand sweeps of expanding circles.

"Rohde is dead."
A fracture in the floor of his mind.
"Rohde."
A crack in the surface ice sheet.
"Dead."
Liquid release. And a tear rolled down his frozen face.

10:00 am – 11:00 am

Early in the evening of December 9, 1868, Professor Friedrich Ritschl sat in his study behind an imposing desk. Constructed for his grandfather at the turn of the century, the desk was made of the finest oak, its dark stain elegantly worn but without a scratch. The leather desk-mat was scuffed on one side, but nowhere torn. In the center of this mat lay a letter-opener; fashioned in the figure of a miniature medieval sword, the blade and scabbard beamed with a bright polish. Stacks of books and papers lined the right side of the desk, just behind an inkwell and pen. In front of these items, a pair of round wire glasses rested atop a folded handkerchief. The book-lined room was immaculate and orderly; even the lamp, reading chair, and side-table in the corner by the door were aligned with mathematical precision in relation to the silk rug in the center of the room. The professor wore a robe draped over a dark suit, his grey hair brushed back above his broad, high forehead. He was well into his sixty-third year, but the curving line of his mouth retained the hint of a youthful smile.

Professor Ritschl had carried home from school several items of light administrative work, letters to read, documents to sign. Now was the time, during a quiet hour before dinner, he had designated for attending to these matters. Therefore after settling himself in his desk-chair, he reached into the central pocket of the leather satchel on the floor beside him, from which he withdrew a small bundle of loose papers and envelopes. He separated the letters into a distinct pile, took up his glasses and wiped the lenses clean with his handkerchief, then wrapping the earpieces behind his ears, he lifted an envelope from the top of the stack. The letter was addressed directly to him, rather than to the administrative office in general, and postmarked from the University of Basel, in Switzerland. He opened it with a deft slice of his little sword. Enclosed he found an appeal for assistance. The department of philology had recently lost a young professor to another university nearer his home, and although they had been granted permission to replace him, they knew of no one qualified for the position. If the honored Herr Professor Ritschl might recommend a suitable candidate, the university would owe him their profoundest gratitude. Etc. etc.

Professor Ritschl leaned back in his chair, intertwined the fingers of his hands, and stared meditatively at the ceiling. "Yes," he thought. "And why not? Doubtless the suggestion would be unprecedented, but it would be just, decidedly the best course of action, and forthright honesty matters most on such occasions as this." Then, sitting forward, he picked up his pen, filled it with ink, and began to write:

Most esteemed Rector Vischer,

Please accept my gratitude for doing me the honor of entrusting me with the role of advisor to your search. I pray I shall not disappoint you. Allow me, therefore, to proceed directly to my point, and to express myself with all due frankness. I have just the man for you. A young man, true, but let this not dissuade you. A young man, moreover, who has not as yet received his degree, nor, *a fortiori*, passed his Habilitation. But, I urge you once more, let this not dissuade you. I have every confidence that our university will not only grant him his doctorate, but will also readily record him as having satisfied the necessary Habilitation requirements, on the basis of the many impressive items of scholarship he has produced and published to date. I assure you: in all my many years of teaching, he is by far the most promising student I have ever had the good fortune to encounter. His fellow students admire him with a wondering awe; and, indeed, I myself consider him a junior peer. As I have said, he is young—a mere twenty-four years old. But he has the natural intellect, the inborn talent, the habituated discipline, and the rigorous training to ensure that he will accomplish any deed to which he ever sets his mind.

The single potential impediment to his continued intellectual growth is his health, which is at times precarious. Assuming, then, that he lives long enough, I foresee for him a brilliant, indeed an unparalleled, future.

I assume you have written to others besides myself, as well you should have done. But, to speak forthrightly, as I must, and as no doubt you would have me do, I assure you that I know of no one in this recent generation of German philologists to compare with this young man, by far the most impressive of my students. Therefore I recommend to you, with enthusiasm, also with the gravity demanded of such a recommendation, my student, Friedrich Nietzsche.

I shall, on a separate page, provide you with the young man's address, as I am certain you shall wish to correspond with him directly, should you decide indeed to interview him, which, again, I encourage you to do.

Please do not hesitate to write to me again if I might be of further assistance. And please know that I am

Yours, sincerely,

Professor Doctor Friedrich Ritschl
Department of Philology
University of Leipzig

***

Twelve years and eight months, almost to the day, after Professor Ritschl penned this recommendation, his former student, the now-retired, solitary, nomadic professor Nietzsche proceeded slowly through the flowering meadow north of Lake Sils, walking away from the Chastè peninsula toward his rented room in the Durisches' little house. He had resurfaced from the depths of his prophetic memory—his prevision, premonition, pre-collection, or pre-recollection: he could not quite hit on the adequate terminology—with his mobility fully restored. Yet he felt somehow out of sorts, somber. Rohde dead? Surely not. He was confident that his old friend yet lived. Still, he felt vaguely as if he moved in a state of mourning. So many friends lost, so many experiences passed through, used up, left behind. "So much, in a way, no longer alive in me."

But what did this mean, really, this "no longer alive in me"? The professor well understood that although his past no longer dwelt in him in the living form it had assumed when present, it inhabited him nonetheless, pulsing through his system as nutrients metabolized and assimilated, the extracted energy animating his every step and thought. His call to Basel, for example. If not for his time at the university there, plodding along for years behind the mask of a scholar, he would not have gathered the stores of psychic energy on which he was presently living, or rather thinking—to him there was little difference. "*Sum, ergo cogito*," he thought to himself. "Ha! Yes, that about sums me up."

Rounding the corner at the Hotel Alpenrose, he paused to look down the lane. He did not want to meet the officious pastor on his way past the church. A local girl knelt to fill a pail at the fountain, but apart from her there was no one around. The girl glanced up when she heard the professor's footfall, and returned his smile. He nodded politely, though he had not intended to smile at her. Was he smiling? Oh, yes, he realized that he was. But he was smiling at himself, and smiling ironically at that, recalling the fact that earlier he had repeatedly addressed the pastor as "father." A natural mistake, perhaps, given his own father's pastoral vocation, coupled with the dream from which he had awoken just hours before encountering the man. Still, the mistake was humorous, or embarrassing, or worrying. Or rather, he thought, it was all of these at once, and more.

Upon thus identifying his psychic state as a composite of contrary emotions, his sister's cry of "Father is dead!" echoed through his mind. But since in his dream that morning he had himself enacted the role of his father, and of his dead brother too, he experienced the words as if they signified "I am dead!" Immediately there welled up in his chest the usual fear of following his father into an early grave, of perhaps even slipping into madness. As fit as he otherwise was, he had inherited a measure of his father's physiological deficiencies, centered, it seemed, behind his eyes, his right eye in particular, and perhaps even in his brain. "But I am stronger than father ever was," he reflected. "My will is stronger, hardened by years of tension that he was spared. The *suddenness* of his illness did him in. He had no preparation for it, no training. Therefore it vanquished him. Haven't I now surpassed him in age?"

And thus began an internal dialogue:

"Yes, I have outlived my father; but not as yet by even a year. Death does not run on a fixed schedule, precise as a Swiss train. Death can wait, even prefers to wait, relishing the shock and surprise frozen on his victim's face."

"True, but if I were destined to succumb to my illness, should I not have done so by now? I bottomed into my lowest state, my weakest condition by far, two years ago in Basel. Yet still I carried on. More, I resisted and overcame. Anyone else in my situation would have given in. But I used my illness to train myself in lightness, goodwill, and joy. I willed myself to cheerfulness, even in the midst of my suffering. I exploited my pain to the end of liberating my thoughts from the petty lure of the here and now, the surface-body and its 'today.' I became a mole; I became a bird. I burrowed beneath the past, soared above the future. I grew subtle, devious, untimely and, therefore, wicked, in the *best* sense of that word."

"Yes, of course I admit the truth of all this. But how to explain these various encroachments of death today, drawing so near, manifesting as dreams, images, feelings, memories, and premonitions even? Why spend this beautiful morning rehearsing the unhappiest episodes of my past, and anticipating those of my future?"

To this final question he had no answer. He felt somehow pregnant, *spiritually* pregnant, but with life or death he could not determine. One's past dies when it transitions into one's present; but through the present it gives birth to one's future, in which it lives on, as a parent lives on in a child. Consider the professor's relation to his own past as a university scholar. He had retired early. He was not presently a professor, nor would he ever again work as a professional academic. Yet for the rest of his wandering life he retained the habit of entering the title 'Professor' in the OCCUPATION column of hotel registries. His scholarly past always informed his self-conception, both in itself and through his perpetual rebellion against it. He had considered abandoning philology even before his call to Basel, but the honor and security of the position were such that he could not decline the offer. Still, he had never fully reconciled himself to the role of scholar-professor.

Following the deaths of his father and brother, he was the sole living male in his immediate family. But he was not as yet an adult. He was far too young to replace his father. He became an adult—a "full grown man," as his sister put it—by way of his post as a university professor, which provided him secure employment, a salary, and public esteem. He was no longer reduced to writing home to beg his mother for money she could not spare; he could now provide for her support. He could introduce his sister into respectable society. He could bear himself at home and abroad with the dignity of one who contributes to society and maintains a family, even if this family comprised a mother and sister rather than a wife and child. Yet despite this improvement in his situation, he had no desire to be a father. All things considered, a family would be a burden, a living distraction from his active mental life. Whenever he thought of marriage, as he did from time to time, he was motivated by fear of loneliness or the anxious need of a helpmeet. Romantic love and the longing for family played no role whatever.

Long ago as a student at Pforta he had developed an affection for Plato's *Symposium*. For a time it was his favorite among Plato's dialogues, and one of his favorite works of all of ancient literature. The dialogue is set in a world of men, an intellectual environment in which women and family play little or no part. And although in the work all sorts of men are included, from doctors to warriors, the scene is dominated by poets and philosophers. At the philosophical summit of the dialogue is a rejection of physical sexual relations in favor of spiritual fatherhood. Hence the expression 'Platonic love,' coined in the Renaissance by Marsilio Ficino, who translated Plato's collected works into Latin. The professor was familiar with Ficino's Florentine Academy, his attempt to reanimate the spirit of Plato's ancient institution in quattrocento Florence. Ficino, too, surrounded himself with intellectual and artistic men; and as he was a priest, and therefore celibate, he advocated, as Plato had done before him, a life of purity and withdrawal from corporeal desire, a life dedicated not to the body but to the soul, to the mind, to philosophical reflection and creative expression. The professor had wanted a secular version of this life for himself, and his vision of such a life had begun to draw him away from institutional philology before the shock of the offer to teach at Basel. In later years he sometimes thought of this shock as having diverted him from his true vocation; at other times he realized that the 'digression' of those ten years was, like the many apparent digressions in Plato's dialogues, not at all a diversion, but rather an element essential to the work that was his life.

At Basel he was extraordinarily busy. He realized almost immediately that his training as a student had hardly prepared him for the effort required to succeed as a professor and scholar. His contract bound him to teach, in addition to his university classes, four lessons every week to students of Greek in the local Pädagogium. Preparing for his classes, which involved the interminable drudgery of meticulous research, the writing of lectures, and the occasional stress of tending to immature or unprepared students, left him little time to concentrate on his own work, which more and more he regarded as philosophical rather than philological. So oppressed was he by the tedium and distraction of his official duties, and so drawn to philosophical reflection, that early in his second year he applied to fill a vacated post in the department of philosophy. His application was denied for lack of formal training in the subject.

Despite the many annoyances involved with his new position, his work did him good—or, rather, he benefitted himself by striving to succeed in it. He developed new strategies for flourishing in difficult conditions. More specifically, he cultivated ingenious routines of self-discipline; he learned to divert his every available resource into his physical and intellectual needs; to extract more productivity from less available time; and to soldier on through frequent bouts of illness and despair. Then there was the content of his teaching. Daily interaction with the pre-Christian, pagan environment of Homer, Aeschylus, Thucydides, and Plato solidified the knowledge he'd acquired during his own years as a student. More, his constant grappling with these and other ancient authors enabled him to deepen his insight into their worlds and worldviews. For instance, he offered regular courses on the Pre-Platonic philosophers and Plato's *Phaedo*, both of which informed his thinking for the rest of his life.

Although he rarely introduced such themes into his lectures, the professor detected in Plato's portrait of the dying Socrates the hyper-rational, naively optimistic, and life-denying features of a spiritual perspective antagonistic to the Greeks' earlier, nobler, tragic view of life, as embodied for example in the best of the Pre-Platonic philosophers. Socrates' aspiration to gather the soul together with itself, alone, separate from the body, and thereby to escape the cycle of rebirth into a ghostly state of eternal existence beyond the heavens, was both a manifestation of, and a factor contributing to, the degeneration of the healthy Archaic Greek spirit into Classical and Hellenistic decadence. Were not Socrates' final words, as recorded in the *Phaedo*, an admission of his corruption?

***

"Who offers sacrifice to Asclepius but one who expects to be cured of an illness?" He spoke to himself as he walked past the church, almost with an urge to sneak by. "Socrates and his sacrificial rooster! This isn't piety. This is decadence! Socrates regarded life as an illness, and death as its cure. But who thinks of life as an illness? Who but one who *suffers* from life, which is to say a *sick man*! Sick at the roots. Not just unhealthy or ill on occasion, as I am, as all men are; but sickly, irremediably prone to sickness, and lacking the reserves of health required to overcome one's sickness, or to overcome oneself by means of it. A fundamentally degenerate type. Rotten physiology."

Now the professor stood once again on the bridge above the Fedacla, where earlier he had lingered recollecting his exchange with Paul Deussen concerning the argument from opposites in Plato's *Phaedo*, the immortal soul, and the motivations of religious belief. As before he leaned against the balustrade, but now he watched the water flowing out of town, winding through the meadow toward Lake Silvaplana.

The local church was just visible in his hazy peripheral vision. The church—oh, yes: earlier he had encountered the pastor immediately upon descending the bridge, and received from him the gift of his eccentric variation on the argument from design for God's existence. "The argument from the beauty of Sils-Maria," the professor christened it. "Well," he joked with himself while meditatively surveying the crystalline stream, the blooming meadow through which it ran, the mountains and sky beyond. "Well, if any such argument were plausible, I suppose I might be persuaded to sympathize with a version invoking the beauty of this place, which has the virtue at least of being undeniable."

The professor then turned and stepped from the bridge, walking toward the Durisches' house. As he approached the front door across the stones laid out on the lawn, he spied Gian Durisch in a downstairs window. The man pressed his face to the glass, waved, disappeared from view, and a moment later opened the front door and greeted the professor with, "Ah, I was only just now anticipating your return, Herr

Professor. Welcome, welcome! A tea for you, sir? Anything at all?"

The professor shook Durisch's outstretched hand and replied, "No, no thank you. Most kind, as always, sir. Most kind indeed. But just now I feel in need of a mid-morning nap." As he spoke he removed his handkerchief and wiped his forehead. "Please do thank your wife again for me, sir. The bread was delicious, as always."

"Oh, of course, of course," Durisch beamed. "Yes, thank *you*. I will certainly pass along your kind words." And glancing at the handkerchief in the professor's hand, he continued, "A long walk this morning, sir? A hike or a climb?"

"No, no," the professor managed a smile. "Only moderate physical activity this morning, friend. But my mind was at work more than usual, or rather it was wandering along unaccustomed byways of thought. Memories, you understand. Recollections and... well, shall we say, foreshadowings. Yes, let's do put it that way, if only so as not to say *over*shadowings. Ha!"

He smiled broadly now, but with a look in his eyes that Durisch could not read. It struck him as somehow distant, distracted; it unnerved him. His conflicted emotions standing as an ox on his tongue, he returned his lodger's smile but remained silent. After a moment the professor spoke again.

"Yes, well then, Herr Durisch. I'll be up to my room now. If you happen to be in, I'd be grateful for a knock at my door in the event you haven't seen me by the lunch hour, or even just a few minutes earlier. You know I prefer to avoid the crowd at the Alpenrose." And with that he took his leave and climbed the stairs to his room.

The professor removed his notebook and pencil from his jacket pocket, hung his jacket on the hook on the back of his door, and started across the room toward the table by the window. But as he moved he was overcome with exhaustion, weak and trembling in the stomach as if he hadn't eaten. He stopped and sat on the side of his bed, and placing his notebook and pencil on the bedside table, he removed his shoes and lay down on his back. He folded his hands across his abdomen and stared at the ceiling, his eyes on the beams of old rough wood overhead, but without consciously attending to them. Thus he fell into his mind, sunk into the well of his thoughts, which were a whirl of images interblending with words and disembodied ideas.

Father. Pastor Merian, "silly fool." His own father erect behind a pulpit. His father writhing and raving in bed. Death, the void. Blindingly bright, abysmally dark. Contraries embracing. Ouroboros. "Rohde and I were joined at the crowns of our heads." Rohde dead? "No, not yet, but already, yes." The dying Socrates condemns life. A rooster beneath the blade for Asclepius, crowing his last. Plato leaps into a tempest stirred up by Heraclitus wrestling with a pair of cosmic judges, each the mirror image of the other. A swirling cloud of dust, spreading, expanding, cosmic, universal, from the center of which there issues a voice, *ego eimi ho ôn*, "I am the existing one." The fury of rushing wind. "I am Being!"

The professor came to with a jolt, as if from falling, and sitting up in bed he reached for his notebook on the nightstand. Then taking up his pencil he opened the notebook to a random page and wrote, *Gott ist todt!* "God is dead!" Then he collapsed on his pillow and fell into a deep sleep.

11:00 am – 12:00 pm

The professor's critique of Plato's portrait of the dying Socrates was grounded on historical research and reflection, but his criticisms were motivated also by more broadly philosophical ideas concerning culture and the role of music in the life of culture. The roots of these latter ideas sprang from the soil of his musical childhood, but they sprouted especially in the period preceding his call to Basel, and flourished in the earliest years of his professorship. The nourishing influence is traceable to the most significant friendship of his life—doomed, like the others, but life-altering in the profoundest sense.

As precocious a pianist and aficionado as young Fritz was, as a child his musical tastes were conventional. He favored the familiar compositions of Mozart, Beethoven, and Haydn. For Christmas and birthdays he received as gifts little bundles of musical scores, sonatas, concertos, and piano reductions of operas and oratorios. With practice he learned to perform these well enough to comprehend them, to understand their structure, their distinctive harmonic colorings and moods. He reposed in the comfortable traditionalism of these works.

Later, as a teenager, Fritz co-founded with two close friends a cultural association dedicated to the study and production of literature, poetry, and music, a group they called 'Germania.' The boys met monthly to share their latest efforts, each member admiring and commenting on his fellows' work. Besides several items of literary and historical commentary and analysis, Fritz contributed his own musical compositions, some based on his inspired improvisations, others conceived with methodical forethought. In keeping with his musical conservatism, his work was accomplished but unadventurous.

When over the course of several meetings one of his fellow Germanians evinced a precocious appreciation for Richard Wagner's so-called *Zukunftsmusik*, even delivering several talks on the subject, Fritz had little patience for it. He could not abide this unusual 'music of the future,' much less his friend's delirious enthusiasm. The sounds made no sense to his ear; the melodies were discordant and jarring. Constantly striving to subvert every orthodox musical piety, this wild music was all too insistently revolutionary. "Is not this outlandish iconoclasm a musical expression of mindless subversion," he interrogated his friend, exasperated. "An objectionable exercise in destruction to no good end? Isn't this all just too unhinged?" As a believer, faithful to the canon and conventional harmonic structure, Fritz quite simply could not understand Wagner's music. Therefore he dismissed it. With the parochial impudence of youth, he resolutely rejected all that was 'modern' in favor of the 'classical,' by which in this context he meant little more than 'familiar.'

In time, however, Fritz succumbed. At twenty-four he lost his head and his heart to Wagner's vision of the future. He was moved in particular by a performance in Leipzig of the Prelude to *Tristan and Isolde* and the Overture to *Die Meistersinger*, after which he declared himself enraptured. His newfound passion was as fervid as his friend's, and eventually his admiration mounted to heights of spiritual euphoria to which few others could ascend. Moreover, not two weeks after his rapturous experience in the Leipzig concert hall, he met and befriended 'the Master' himself. His enthusiasm was boundless. Later still, however, he would come to reject all things, and indeed most all people, having to do with Wagner.

But before the dismal winter of the death of their companionship, the springtime of their happiness blossomed with love and mutual understanding. Who would have expected it? So coincidental were the circumstances of their first meeting, so absurd the immediate events leading up to it, and so inspiring and bewildering the occasion itself, that Fritz later described the episode as seeming like a fiction, a farce, an idyll, and a dream.

It happened that in the autumn of 1868, Wagner was visiting his sister incognito in Leipzig. And it happened that this sister was the wife of a Leipzig professor, himself the colleague of Fritz's Professor Ritschl. It also happened that Frau Professor Ritschl, having been invited to dinner to meet the great man, upon hearing him play a selection from one of his works, mentioned that she was familiar with the piece by way of a young philologist of her acquaintance, her husband's brightest pupil, who was moreover a talented pianist and passionate Wagnerian. Intrigued, Wagner requested to meet this young man. "We shall have him round for dinner," he announced, according to his habit of dictating the affairs of every house he visited. "My work, my *mission*, requires the assistance of intelligent young men and women willing, and able, to spread the good word, *bold* enough for the task, you understand. Moreover, my hectic life leaves me so little time to speak with really *knowledgeable* people. And as my mind thrives on activity, learning, and expansion, I often feel so terribly *bereft*, deprived, as I am, of good, noble, cultured, truly *erudite* company. And needless to say, of course, what better intellectual society might one wish than the company of a man with a passion for both the *best* music and the *Greeks* as well! A man after my own heart, truly! Yes, I should like very much to meet this young man. Tomorrow, then, it is—yes, tomorrow or Sunday. Whichever may be most convenient, of course. Do arrange it, sister." And after holding forth in this way, the maestro resumed his playing, whistling and singing the various accompanying vocal lines himself.

The day after this gathering, Fritz returned home from a morning stroll surprised to find a note at his door inviting him to visit the following day at the home of Professor Brockhaus, with whom he was only slightly acquainted through Professor Ritschl. Reading further, his surprise swelled into a stunned stupefaction when he learned that the maestro Richard Wagner would be there too, and that, moreover, the man himself had personally requested his attendance. His fingers went limp and the letter dropped to the floor, spinning in fluttering circles. He stared down at the note as at a gift descended from the heavens, but his poor vision impeded his eager efforts to verify the small, hand-printed contents as it lay there at his feet. Therefore he knelt down to retrieve the note, and after reading it through once again, he sat on the edge of his bed in wonder and amazement. His first thought was: Oh, God, what shall I wear?!

As it happened, Fritz had recently placed an order with a local tailor for a new evening suit. It was due to be ready any day. By tomorrow? Perhaps! He folded the precious invitation and slid it carefully into its envelope, rose from his bed and laid it precisely in the center of his desk. Then he bolted from the house and ran the three blocks to the tailor's shop.

"No, sir, I am sorry to inform you that your suit is not yet ready, sir," the tailor announced, with a note of sincere regret in his voice. "I am, however, close to finally accomplishing the task, very nearly done indeed. In fact, sir, I have it here in my book—look here, you see, sir, you see?—I have it right here to be done on the morrow, and, indeed, I have just this morning scheduled my most responsible man to deliver it directly to your residence tomorrow afternoon. Yes, look sir, you see, I have the date and time right here, inscribed by my own hand! I really cannot complete my work to your satisfaction today, sir. Of course I hate to disappoint you, sir, of course I do. But, that is to say, will a delivery tomorrow be terribly inconvenient to you, sir?"

Fritz replied that any time early the following afternoon would be convenient, but that he really could not accept the suit any later, for he had a most important engagement scheduled that very evening. After receiving the tailor's assurance that he would present him with a fine suit—"fine, sir, very fine, most elegant indeed!"—he returned to his apartment in a wandering, wondering, dreamlike state.

***

The following morning dawns grimly, dark skies rumbling low overhead, sleet and occasional bursts of snow blanket Leipzig with a grey slush. Fritz is impatient for the hours to pass. He tries to read but cannot concentrate. Tries to write, to no avail. He would like to rush to the tailor's shop to check on the man's progress, to hurry him along with his work. But this would be futile, he knows, little more than occasion for struggling against high winds, and likely catching a cold. He is grateful for the distraction, then, when at two o'clock a friend, a doctoral candidate in philosophy, stops by as scheduled to explain the Eleatic philosophy of Being and the One, as expressed obscurely in Parmenides' poem and Plato's equally abstruse dialogue, *Parmenides*. They discuss and debate these matters, and the philosophical concept of God in general, for two full hours, Fritz persistently interrogating his friend with puzzled exasperation and penetrating worries and objections. For a while he almost loses himself in the conversation, but on hearing a bell chime the hour outside, he sees through the window the darkness of evening descending. Where is that tailor's man?! Where is his suit?! Now his plans in every detail flood back into his mind, drowning out all other thoughts. Therefore he excuses himself, hurries his friend out the door, and paces his room impatiently, wondering what he will wear to dinner if he does not receive his suit on time.

But then a sound through the window! Maybe. A call, a voice? It is hard to distinguish through the pebbling noise of the falling sleet. There! Was that wind in the trees or a human voice crying, "Ho there, sir!"? He looks through the window but sees nothing. Then he presses his face against the pane and blocks the glare of the interior light with a hand cupped over his eyes. Yes, there by the back gate—which is inexplicably locked!—a shadow, a figure, a man holding an umbrella aloft in one hand, a large box under his other arm.

"There's my man, at last!" Fritz hurries out into the weather and ushers the man inside, where pausing on the doormat he stamps his feet while furiously brushing the water from his hair and shoulders. Then, as he leads the delivery-man up to his room, he grabs the box, discards the lid on the floor in the hall, and begins to remove the suit. Thanking the man as they enter the room, he places the box on his bed, laying beside it the jacket he has by now fully removed from the enfolding tissue; and while undoing the buttons of his shirt with one hand, with the other he takes the delivery-man by the elbow, escorts him to the door, and bids him give the tailor his best. But as he turns around to change, he senses that the man has not left the room. He looks over his shoulder, a quizzical look on his face.

"Yes, what is it man? I believe I have thanked you, and the good tailor too. Please, then, be on your way. And a good evening to you."

But the man will not leave. He requests payment for the suit. Fritz is taken aback. "Sir," he is speaking firmly now. "Sir, I am afraid you misunderstand the situation. I shall pay the tailor himself, of course, as would any gentlemen. But I shall not provide payment to his hireling. Who would think of such a thing, really?"

But the man insists. Then Fritz insists. He turns away again and takes up the jacket intending to try it on, expecting the man will leave if he ignores him. But as he crosses the room toward the mirror, the man takes hold of a loose sleeve and attempts to pull the jacket from his hands. He tugs at the sleeve with surprising vigor, and while doing so he spins around to face the bed, reaching out with his free hand toward the box.

"Really, man," Fritz is shouting now. "Really, would you seize my property by force?! Shall I send for an authority to have you removed?! This is theft! Really, this is unbearable, man, quite simply unpardonable!"

But the delivery-man will not desist, and his silent perseverance is unsettling. Fritz is still young, inexperienced in worldly affairs, and he begins to fear the man. "Well, then, sir," he says, affecting a measure of composure. "If you simply must persist in this outrageous behavior, I do not know what else to do than leave you be, sunk in your own crassness. Let your bad behavior be your chastisement, I say! A vicious man is his own punishment. But I shall certainly make a point of having a stern word with your employer tomorrow morning!"

And with these words he sits down on his bed and watches the man depart, taking the suit with him. He is dumbfounded. He is almost in tears. He pounds a fist against his thigh so hard it hurts. Then, after some moments surrendering to this state of angry bewilderment, he pulls himself together, dresses in an old but respectable dark suit, and sits down at his desk. He still has time to spare, and he is determined to relax and collect his thoughts before leaving. He allows himself twenty minutes to sit still and breathe, eyes closed, head down, the palms of his hands resting on his thighs.

When finally he has calmed down, and his heart rate and temperature have returned to normal, he consults the clock: twenty minutes exactly! But now he must leave or else he will overheat from rushing to arrive on time. Downstairs in the foyer he takes an umbrella from the stand and pauses to examine his appearance in the hallway mirror. Then he steps out into the night.

He hasn't far to walk, only seven blocks to a lane on the other side of the city center. And since immediately upon his setting out the sleet and snow retreat to a fine drizzle, he makes good time without hurrying. He arrives at the door of the Brockhaus home only five minutes late, which he assures himself will be no mark against him, and perhaps even a point in his favor. Taking a moment to collect his thoughts under the glow of the gaslight, he places his umbrella in the stand among several others, then he smooths his jacket with both hands, scrutinizes his reflection in the window beside the door, and grips the heavy brass knocker and lets it fall. As he awaits a response he hears gay laughter and voices inside, accompanied by bright chords struck on the piano. He imagines the evening ahead of him and is eager to enter, excitedly shifting his weight from one foot to the other, very nearly in the style of a jig. He knows he must cut a ridiculous figure, but he cannot help himself. He is vibrating with anticipation. Then, upon hearing footsteps through the door, he interrupts his frantic dance and stands at attention. Frau Professor Brockhaus herself swings open the door, and recognizing him as the only guest not yet present, she greets him warmly and escorts him into the presence of the master.

"Ah, so *you're* the brilliant young Wagnerian philologist, are you?" says Wagner in a booming voice, rising from the piano bench and striding toward the young man awestruck in the center of the room, straining to keep the muscles of his face from quivering. "Let's have a look at you then! Come, come." And taking Fritz by the hand he shakes it vigorously, then slaps him on the shoulder and leads him to the divan, settling himself in a reading chair opposite.

The interrogation begins immediately, with Wagner inquiring about his reputation among the academics, the origin of Fritz's interest in his music, probing the breadth of his knowledge and the depth of his devotion. Only after he has satisfied his curiosity regarding these details does he ask Fritz about himself, his intellectual interests and research. What, for example, does he intend for the subject of his dissertation? And what are his plans afterward? Will he write? Will he teach? As self-absorbed as he is, he is nonetheless sincerely interested. This is evident from the attention he pays to his interlocutor's every word, the care he takes in his replies, the memory he retains of every statement uttered. Taking note of this, Fritz is impressed. But before he can speak at length of himself and his future aspirations, Frau Professor Brockhaus summons the guests to table for dinner.

The party lingers over the meal for well over an hour, their eating frequently interrupted by Wagner's protracted monologues, his ribald jokes and outrageous mockeries of stuffy academics and hidebound German musical taste. But the minutes seem to Fritz to pass as seconds. Dinner is a blur of movement and sound; he hardly notices the taste of the food.

After dinner the guests return to the living room, where Wagner regales them with selections from his autobiography, modulating his delivery to suit the scenes, from maudlin sentimentality to blustering burlesque. Then, having had his fill of his authorial self, he lays his papers on a table and resumes playing the piano.

"Come, *come* young man," he calls to Fritz. "Come near and keep an old man company, son." He means to be joking about his age, for, as he well knows, and as is evident to anyone ever in his presence, every movement of his body and mind is infused with the vibrant agility of youth. But as Fritz stands up and approaches the man, he recalls from his reading that Wagner was born the same year as his father, only five months earlier in fact. For a moment, viewed from the back while seated at the piano, he even has the look of the paternal pastor, the same dark hair and sloping shoulders. Fritz stands beside him and studies his profile. No striking similarities there. But when Wagner looks up at him while playing, laughs and winks his eye, he is Father for that one second, and that second sinks into Fritz's soul, an eternal second that quivers and flows but never passes, never blinks out of existence.

Later in the evening, after a few of the other guests have departed and voices are quieter, Fritz decides that he too should leave. He does not want to overstay his welcome. But as he determines to announce his intention to go, and to thank his hosts for a wonderful evening, Wagner speaks up and asks his opinion of Schopenhauer. "He's no Hellene, I understand," he jokes, "and therefore no matter for one's *professional* attention. And of course the professional professors despise him with a passion, with a *fever*. Ha! But to me—ah, to me Schopenhauer is the world," he muses, his eyes cast dramatically heavenward. "Yes, to me old Schopenhauer is *everything*. He is, you know, the only philosopher to grasp in full the true significance of music—the *metaphysical* significance, you understand." He then proceeds to discourse of Schopenhauer in some detail, with enthusiasm and a layman's erudition. He is delighted to learn that Fritz not only admires Schopenhauer too, but that he is well acquainted with his work, even has novel insights into Schopenhauer's relation to Greek tragic culture, which he describes to the master in terms of a deep, almost mystical metaphysic that he refers to as "the Dionysian *Weltanschauung*." Wagner is intrigued, eager to press the discussion further; but by now it is late, and his sister has let it be known that the evening must be winding down. Wagner smiles at her protectiveness, disappointed to interrupt his conversation, but grateful for her solicitations. Nodding to his new young friend, he rises from his seat and thanks the remaining guests for a delightful evening, which is his way of permitting them to leave. Fritz stands up in turn and offers his warmest appreciation to his hosts, then reaches out to shake Wagner's hand. The master, smiling broadly, pushes his hand aside, throws an arm around his shoulder and walks him to the door.

"We really must meet again, son. We haven't yet *nearly* done speaking of Schopenhauer, and I would very much like to hear more about this *Dionysian* worldview—the Greeks and their tragedies, as surely you know, being of particular interest to me. So, please do write or pay us a visit. My sister will let you know my whereabouts, I'm sure. Indeed, I shall *encourage* her to do so. At the moment we reside in Switzerland, near Lucerne. A beautiful place, really! Quite *mythological*, if you will. Good, so, until then, my new young friend. And good evening to you, a good evening indeed!"

Standing outside on the Brockhauses' porch, Fritz is overcome. He takes a moment to catch his breath, to assure himself that the evening has actually transpired, in reality rather than in a dream; then he wanders off down the sidewalk, leaving his umbrella in the stand by the door.

The weather having long since passed out of town, the sky is cloudless overhead; and as Fritz walks he frequently stops to stare up at the stars, laughing in delighted disbelief at his own good fortune. And to think of the absurd events that preceded the evening! Oh, that delivery-man and his suit! He worried the affair might be a bad omen, though he does not believe in portents or signs. Still, he was genuinely apprehensive, for he so wanted the evening to succeed. Well, it was better than he ever could have hoped, better than he could have imagined. An invitation to visit the master himself, and in Switzerland! To discuss Schopenhauer and the Greeks in private with the master himself! No, he could not have wished for anything more from the evening! In this way he babbles to himself walking home, paying no attention to the route but finding his way by habit nonetheless.

It is late as he approaches the gate surrounding the property around his building, and it occurs to him that the entry might be locked, as earlier it had been locked against the delivery-man. What a scene that was! And of course in the aftermath he left his apartment without his keys! He laughs at his distraction, amused at the various peripeteias of the day, laughs despite himself and the present potential inconvenience. Fortunately, the gate is unlatched. But what of the door to the building?! Of course it is locked! He is certain he does not have the keys. He pictures them on his desk beside the precious invitation. The ironic juxtaposition evokes more laughter. He searches his pockets in vain, then searches them through once more, not at all expecting to find the keys. But what else can he do? At this hour he has nowhere else to go. He can only laugh, which he does, yet again; and he knocks at the door, hoping to arouse a ground-floor tenant from bed. But no; no one comes. So there he stands, laughing at his predicament, knocking on the door, laughing and knocking, knocking and laughing. Ha, ha ha! Knock, knock, knock! Ha, ha, ha! Knock, knock, knock!

***

The professor awoke from his nap to the sound of Herr Durisch knocking on his door.

"Herr Professor, sir." Durisch spoke in a low voice, his face pressed against his lodger's door. "Sir, it is I, Durisch. You requested that I call to wake you before lunch. Are you awake, Herr Professor? Do you hear me?"

The professor blinked and shook his head, took a moment to come to his senses, then sat up and replied, "Mm, yes. Yes, Herr Durisch. Thank you. I am awake now. Thank you indeed! I seem to have overslept, but I am now quite awake. I shall be down soon. Thank you."

Relieved, Durisch moved to withdraw, but before turning away he inquired, "Forgive me, sir. But are you quite alright in there? I thought I heard you moaning, or perhaps even laughing, as I knocked. You *are* well, sir, are you not?"

"Oh, yes," the professor assured him, smiling to himself. "Yes, yes. I believe I was dreaming. Was I laughing? Ha! Imagine that! Well, it was after all a happy dream! Yes, a most happy dream of my youth!"

12:00 pm – 1:30 pm

Passing by the church on his way to lunch at the Alpenrose, the professor heard the lilting sounds of piano music circulating behind the closed front door. It reminded him of his first visit to Wagner's home in Tribschen. A few months after the wondrous gathering at the Brockhaus residence in Leipzig, Fritz was surprised by the call to Basel, another happy coincidence, for the city was a mere two hours by train from Lucerne, the metropolis of Tribschen. He had been encouraged again to visit Wagner by a New Year's greeting card posted by the man himself, a kindness Fritz had not expected, and which delighted him. He assumed his teaching duties in May of 1869, and on the Saturday morning of his first long weekend he made the trip to Tribschen. Wagner's villa stood alone in an idyllic setting—"mythological," as he recalled the maestro having put it—elegant atop the rise of a mossy green hill overlooking Lake Lucerne, with a view of the lake itself, several surrounding forested hills, and mountains in the distance. The sky was a dazzling ethereal blue. As his visit was unannounced, he had no idea whether anyone would be home; but when he approached the door and heard the piano echoing within, he was certain the master was in. The servant who responded to the bell attempted to rush him off, but immediately thereafter Wagner himself turned up, delighted to see him.

"Ah, splendid!" he gushed, dismissing his servant with an affectionate slap on the shoulder. "Our young philologist has arrived at last! A *splendid* surprise indeed!"

Unfortunately, however, the maestro was just then hard at work composing, and he required a weekend of uninterrupted concentration. But as the family would be free for the Monday holiday, he invited Fritz to return that day for lunch.

Returning to Lucerne, Fritz rented a comfortable room from which he sallied out on sightseeing adventures around the town, impatiently awaiting Monday and the occasion to converse with Wagner. In the evening he settled into a large chair by the window of his room, taking notes of grammatical problems in the text of Plato's *Phaedo*, which he was reading at the time with students of Greek at the Basel Pädagogium. As he studied the work he puzzled over Plato's subversions of the oppositions he himself introduced between *logos* and *mythos*, fact and fiction, reason and the irrational. Socrates explicitly contrasted himself with the poets as a man concerned with arguments rather than fables, but then he spoke in fables, described his *logoi* as *mythoi*, and even employed the word *mythologein* with reference to his own intellectual activities, a word that joined the apparent contraries *mythos* and *logos* into a unity, Heraclitus style. He was struck even more than on previous readings by Plato's depicting Socrates himself as remarking that his arguments for immortality were incomplete, and susceptible to other objections as well. He took note of these peculiarities, and he wondered about their implications for Socrates' confident assertions that at death his soul would finally escape the prison-house of his body to live forever liberated from corporeal bondage. Were these claims not meant to be true? But why offer sacrifice to Asclepius, god of healing, if death after all was no cure? Was Socrates really a philosopher, or was he rather an artist? Or was Plato the artist at work here, deceiving with a good conscience, playfully but subtly undermining the oppositions on which the arguments of his character Socrates were grounded?

These questions were well outside the scope of the professor's elementary lessons in Greek grammar, and they were most likely beyond the consideration of even the best of his university students, with whom anyway he was reading the tragedies of Aeschylus, not Plato's dialogues. But he did raise the subject with Wagner after lunch on the Monday of his "first officially recorded visit" (Fritz's own expression) to Tribschen. Wagner was an excellent conversationalist—when, that is, he wasn't indulging his passion for his own ideas by way of extended monologues. He thought deeply about the nature of the artist and the form and substance of the artist's creations; but as he knew little in detail about Plato, he found it difficult to situate the dialogues in this aesthetic context. He was much more interested in his young friend's thoughts on the Greek tragedians, the "Dionysian *Weltanschauung*" he had mentioned during their first meeting, and the bearing of these matters on his own life and work. Fritz was happy to humor Wagner's whims and inclinations, to tailor his speech to suit the master's particular interests, but as they spoke of the tragic worldview, he kept in mind his developing thoughts about Plato and Socrates.

Fritz called on Wagner many times throughout his first summer in Basel. He befriended Wagner's wife, too, Cosima, who respected and admired him in return. He was even present when she gave birth to Wagner's first son, named Siegfried after the music-drama the master was then composing, the third of the four parts of his epic 'Ring of the

Nibelung' cycle. He was there, too, on Christmas morning the following year when Wagner surprised his wife by mustering a small orchestra at the foot of the stairs leading up to her bedroom to perform the *Tribschen Idyll*, his musical holiday gift composed especially for the occasion. Cosima was still asleep when the musicians began to play, so—and this was by design—she awoke to the sound of swelling music rising up in celebration of her, of her husband's love for her, and of the fruit of their love, Siegfried.

At home with the Wagners personally and intellectually, Fritz not only visited regularly, but when there he read to the couple his latest essays, which generated ever increasing intensities of excitement, stimulating long evenings of conversation, for his ideas seemed almost to rise as steam from an intoxicating brew of scholarship and visionary insight, always novel, always penetrating, and relevant to the contemporary scene, despite being rooted in reflections on the ancient world.

***

The lunch staff at the Alpenrose knew the professor by sight. Usually the woman in charge of the tables led him to his seat, even when he arrived early to a nearly empty room, as he preferred to do, but especially when he arrived on time, or late, and the tables were already crowded. She had learned from previous interactions that his eyesight was poor, and that he was anxious when negotiating unfamiliar or congested rooms. He could manage on his own by now, having taken his lunch here many times, but still he preferred to be seated and served; the fewer distractions the better. He waited at the door upon entering the room, disappointed to be later than usual.

"Ah, Herr Professor, welcome!" The woman in charge of the room approached him, smiling, her arm outstretched to usher him to his usual table, around which sat only two other diners. "Welcome! I see you're running late today, sir. But not too late—not at all. You've anticipated the arrival of the bulk of our guests, I'm sure."

The professor nodded to the woman and smiled, following her to his seat. "Thank you, Fräulein," he said. "You are well today, I trust? I'm sorry to have missed you yesterday, but I hiked up through Val Fex and was really quite exhausted on my return. I believe I collapsed and fell asleep immediately upon entering my room, and when I finally woke the time for lunch had long fled."

The woman smiled as she pulled out his chair and placed a cloth napkin on the table. "Well, you certainly are looking refreshed today, sir, if you don't mind my saying so. Yes, I suppose that yesterday you took the sun on your cheeks, for your face has the glow of a healthy young man."

"Ha! You flatter me Fräulein, as usual," he replied, taking his seat and smiling up at the woman. "But as usual I appreciate your kindness."

Returning his smile, she inquired whether he would like meat and macaroni to eat, which she expected he would as he'd never once requested anything else; then she hurried off to prepare his plate and pour him a large glass of water.

The professor ate slowly, quietly, keeping his body very still. He lowered his head to avoid catching anyone's eye, for he did not like to be drawn into frivolous exchanges with strangers. Fortunately, the woman had earlier seated his fellow diners at the far end of the table, anticipating his arrival. She knew he preferred empty chairs between himself and others, if such an arrangement were at all possible, as it was at this phase of the lunch service. As he ate he allowed his mind to wander, concentrating on the flow of his thoughts to block out the chatter and noise of the room. There were times when he enjoyed overhearing talk of current events, the various outrages of government and public scandal, and occasionally even engaging strangers in conversations regarding contemporary life and mores, for as little interest as he had in such matters in and for themselves, he studied them as symptoms of the health of European culture. His diagnosis was always the same: *sick*. But today he withdrew from the circumambient clamor into the silence of his own mind.

His thoughts moved slowly at first, matching the pace of his digestion, but when he broke a corner from the bread in a basket beside his plate, the day's two dreams emerged from his subconsciousness to occupy his full attention. He reviewed the details of the dreams themselves and the effects they'd had on his intellect and mood. Together they had carried him back to the lowest and the highest points of his life to date. "My abyss and my summit," he thought, "my midnight and my noon." But why? Why should his subconscious mind occupy itself with these things today, and why disturb his conscious awareness with them? He tried but could not imagine a lower point than the death of his father, except perhaps his own early death or living descent into madness; but in the event, he reasoned, the incident would not be a new and worse occurrence, but rather a continuation and exacerbation of the original episode. His dead father lived in him; and his own death would be his father's living act. "A strange formulation, that," he reflected, looking up from his plate at nothing in particular. "My dead father's living act. A strange formulation, indeed. Yet it strikes me as accurate—as really quite perfectly and precisely accurate." He took up his napkin and touched it to his mouth, then replaced it in his lap. He looked at the glass of water before him, reached out and wrapped his fingers around it; but he did not pick it up. Seated thus, with one hand relaxed in his lap, the other gripping his water glass, he withdrew again into his mind.

As for the dream of his happiest days, in a sense he judged it impossible to experience a higher joy than had been his during his years of intimacy with Wagner. The fact that the two had since fallen out, and had exchanged no words of kindness for years, neither in person nor in writing, did not affect his estimation. In another sense, however, which it now occurred to him might well be a deeper sense, every moment of his life was a summit and a bright midday. Anyway, he thought, it should be so; certainly he should strive to make it so. Yes, even this very moment, sitting here in the Alpenrose, eating this food, drinking this water, and thinking these very thoughts. Was this moment not good? Was it not great? It was *his* moment, after all; and thus in a way it was *him*. "There is no duality here," he reasoned, "no separation between an 'I' and a 'now,' no isolated moment occupied by a discretely individuated ego. There is only the 'I-now.' Or, no: even this compound is too limited, too limiting, individuating. Rather there is only the, let's say, only the 'unbounded-ongoing.' Ha, yes! That's it! There is, in short," he continued, "there is only the continuum, the flux, the river. But to the extent that a ripple on water can be conscious of itself (and for now I'll imagine it so), even though it is ephemeral and ontologically indistinct from the river, it can at least say 'Yes!' to itself, both as itself and as the river of which it is but a transient mode. If this is so, then there can be no happiest moment of a life, no one happy moment above all others. Each and every moment thrills with the highest possible happiness—or rather, a man must transform every moment into his highest and happiest noon by *affirming* it as such. Only thus can one affirm the whole of one's life, the pleasures and the pains alike. And what after all are pleasure and pain but insignificant epiphenomena, sparks cast off from the excitation of nerves, and by no means the standard and measure of things. The 'Yes!' penetrates deeper than this, rises higher as well—and carries one up on its wings. And haven't I said that I want one day to be only a Yes-sayer?"

The professor had long been occupied with the 'Yes!' that expresses the affirmation of life, the value, as well as the difficulty, of pronouncing it from the deepest wells of self-regarding goodwill. But in recent years the matter had weighed even more heavily on his mind, for he had come to regard affirmation as an act of defiance in the face of his own unremitting outbreaks of illness, a test and a proof of his underlying health and potency, also as a form of therapy, his philosophical cure for the surface layers of sickness that periodically harassed him. A fundamentally unhealthy man would long since have succumbed to the extreme eruptions of illness that had assaulted him throughout his life, and ravaged him with even crueler severities for the last five years. A weaker man would lose heart, break down, and allow his condition to take its course until finally it did him in. But the professor resisted, indefatigable in his quest to map the route to the summit of joy through the abyss of pain. Thus he turned his creative and well-trained mind to studying the existential preconditions of affirmation, to analyzing the spiritual meaning of the great 'Yes!' to life, and to training himself to acquire the power to speak it, to shout it, to sing and to dance it.

The professor had recorded his initial thoughts about these matters in a book he wrote early in his time at Basel. *The Birth of Tragedy Out of the Spirit of Music*, he called it, his first book, his introduction to the world of European scholarly culture. And what a shocking introduction it was! More like a portrait in prose of a seer's vision than a sober academic treatise, the book was an eccentric amalgamation of historical analysis, cultural critique, Schopenhauerian metaphysics, and homage to the genius of his new friend and mentor, Wagner.

The historical, cultural, and aesthetic origins of Greek tragic theater had been a subject of speculation at least since Aristotle's day, and most likely even earlier. In his own work the young professor traced tragedy as an art-form back to a transient period of synchronizing confluence between two generally antagonistic forces operative within the Greek psyche, forces he designated 'Apollonian' and 'Dionysian.' Apollo was the god of reason and order, of sobriety and serenity, as expressed for example in the measure of harmony, poetic meter, and comprehensible dramatic narrative. Apollo the god of light. Dionysus was Apollo's opposite, the god of darkness and intoxication, the genius of musical abandon and the wild, unrestrained dance. The forces represented by these two gods infused and informed the Hellenic spirit, permeating the Greeks' cultural and political institutions, their art, their distinctive tendencies of thought and modes of life.

Considering these forces as manifest in an individual, particularly in the artist, the professor portrayed the man possessed by Dionysus as exploding the constraints of his rational mind, penetrating the veil of multiplicity that constitutes the world of appearances, and unifying with the vital force that pulses through the core of things, the Schopenhauerian Will to Live that exists at, and as, the singular root of reality.

Faithfully following Schopenhauer, the professor depicted the Will to Live as insatiable in its violence, a relentless will that devours itself for nourishment, annihilates itself for generation, a will, in short, whose life is death and whose death is life. Therefore the Dionysian man, lost in his enthusiastic frenzy, who for a moment *is* the Will to Live incarnate, experiences in himself the violence and suffering inherent in the will's self-consuming life-force. But in this moment *as* life *willing* life, infused with the spirit and strength of his god, he says 'Yes!' to life, and thereby affirms, even redeems, himself and all the world.

Socrates was born into the "tragic age of the Greeks," but he grew up to reject the tragic *Weltanschauung*. He was the paradigmatically anti-Dionysian man, a single-minded disciple of Apollonian rationality, harmony, and order. He could neither endure suffering nor accept the thought that the world is inherently irrational. Therefore he taught the great 'No!' to life as it is, regarding it as his duty "to heal the eternal wound of existence," and for this he prescribed knowledge as the *pharmakon*. Believing that humans suffer because of their vices, and that they are vicious because they are ignorant, Socrates reasoned that knowledge will lead them to virtue and thereby generate happiness. There is, then, a cure for human suffering, namely, Reason.

When the Athenians executed Socrates, they made him a martyr to this anti-tragic, life-denying perspective. The dying Socrates became a symbol of Reason as cure for the ills of life so seductive it appealed to hordes of Athenian youth, foremost among them Plato, who promoted his master's knowledge-therapy in his dialogues, and memorialized the dying Socrates specifically in the *Phaedo*. The tragic age of the Greeks was eventually displaced by the ever-expanding influence of a Platonism infused with Socrates' therapeutic rationalism, which spread throughout the Mediterranean and nourished the soil out of which Christianity emerged to preach its own gruesome 'No!' to life.

Apart from providing this historical-philosophical account of the rise and fall of Greek tragic culture, the professor's book was a bold appeal for the modern renewal of the tragic spirit and Dionysian life affirmation. For two thousand years Platonic and Christian dogma had taught men to deny the beauty of the real world—violent, irrational, and full of suffering, but beautiful and real—and diverted their longing to another world, an after-world of disembodied eternal bliss. But this 'world' is a delusion, ugly and unreal. As eruptions of the ancient spirit into modern life, Wagner's music-dramas challenged the Platonic-Christian deception and cleared the way for cultural renewal, for a rebirth of tragedy, and, perhaps, for a return of the tragic 'Yes!' to life. In recognition of Wagner's example, the professor dedicated his book to him.

***

Boom! Clang! The professor was aroused from his distracted state by the striking sounds of silverware, plates, and teacups clattering, diners conversing and laughing, boots and heels clacking against the hardwood floor, the dragged legs of chairs scraping and clapping. He looked up to see the dining-hall nearly full of patrons. Surprised, he wondered at the strangeness of the passage of time, for it seemed the room had filled up in a moment he hadn't notice pass, so instantaneous was its movement; yet it also seemed an eternity since he'd last looked up from his plate. Hadn't he been away, in Basel, writing at his desk? Hadn't he been in the Wagners' drawing room, reading a draft of his book aloud? Hadn't he also been a spectator in the theater of Dionysus, sitting at the base of the Acropolis in Athens, under the sun, intoxicated, possessed by a vision of the god in the form of masked men singing and dancing on the orchestra floor? But hadn't he only a moment before replaced his napkin in his lap and reached out for his water glass, around which his fingers were still enfolded?

The professor reflected on these questions as he finished his meal and drank his water. Then the woman who had seated him approached and knelt beside him. "Herr Professor," she spoke in a soft voice. "I see that you've almost finished your meal. Are you well? I noticed you sitting quite frozen for a time as the other guests came and went, but I didn't like to disturb you. Is anything the matter? Are you all right?" She stood up to await his answer, smiling reassuringly, her hand on the back of his chair.

"Oh, Fräulein, yes. Yes, you're quite right," he replied. "I seem to have lost myself in a labyrinth of time. But, no, nothing at all is the matter, I assure you. In fact I feel quite well, quite well indeed." And smiling up at her he added, "But I do appreciate your attentive concern. You are most kind."

"May I remove your plate then, sir?" she asked, in reply to which he smiled and pushed back his chair. "Thank you, Fräulein," he said, standing up and nodding. "Yes, thank you. Until tomorrow, then. Arrivederla!" Then he left the room and headed back to the Durisches' house.

Gian Durisch was working in the front yard when the professor approached. "A good meal, I hope," he called out for a greeting, setting down his trowel and wiping the palms of his hands on his pants.

"Yes, the usual," the professor replied, smiling. "And you know I crave regularity in such things. I find the sameness somehow comforting, and, besides, the repetition is good for my system, which doesn't take well to sudden alterations of routine."

"Are you in for the day then?" Durisch asked. "Or have you returned for what I once heard called a postprandial nap? Ha!"

"Very good, Herr Durisch," the professor laughed. "Yes, 'postprandial' indeed. Not quite the purest of Latin, that; but very good nonetheless. But, anyway, no—I've had my fill of sleeping for the day. I believe I'll just relax for a little, perhaps write a letter home to my family. Then I'll step out for my afternoon walk to the far shore of Silvaplana. The weather is especially fine today," he added. "A cloudless sky and not too hot. An ideal afternoon for walking and ruminating outdoors!"

Upstairs in his room, the professor hung his jacket up and sat down at the table under the window. He gazed out at the trees beside the house and the path that disappeared among their shadows. Then cupping his chin and cheek in his left hand, he relaxed to allow his mind to wander and trailed his thoughts as they ran back to his blissful early years with Wagner. A few months after the publication of his *Birth of Tragedy*, Wagner's own aesthetic aspirations came to fruition. Over the course of several years the maestro had solicited funds from scores of donors, saving to finance an opera house dedicated to his work. By the spring of 1872 he had finally collected capital sufficient to begin construction. The Festspielhaus would stand in Bayreuth, to which town the Wagners had relocated, leaving their home in Tribschen for good. Wagner had arranged a ceremony around the laying of the theater's foundation stone, inviting to the event a gaudy coalition of financial contributors, honored guests, and musicians from every region of Europe. Speeches would be delivered, music performed, meals served, parties thrown. It was a cultural celebration in the grand style, precisely the sort of extravagant affair which Wagner excelled at producing.

The ceremonial placement of the stone was conducted on the morning of Wagner's fifty-ninth birthday. With guests gathered round on all sides, the composer approached the site in a carriage, the festive strains of an ensemble ushering him along. It was a glorious occasion, radiant with the promise of cultural rejuvenation, one of the high points of Wagner's life. And accompanying the great man in his carriage, a cherished participant in the celebration, was his friend and keen disciple, the academic and author, thinker and walker, philologist and budding philosopher—yes, there beside the master sat his favorite young intellectual, overjoyed and marveling at his fate.

These were the days before the professor's insight that a man must aspire to affirm every moment of his life, to transform all events into sources of his highest happiness. Sitting across from Wagner in the carriage that morning, he was certain he would never again experience such rapturous heights of joy. He seriously considered resigning from Basel to dedicate his life to promoting Wagner and his work. Little did he know that soon he would derive only sorrow from the relationship, and that in time his brightest memories of Wagner would be obscured by shadows as dark as those among the trees outside the window through which he now sat staring, alone in a rented room with only the shades of friendships past for company.

1:30 pm – 3:00 pm

My dear mother,

Perched up here 6000 feet above the north Italian plain, one cannot expect an eternal spring. Indeed, only a fool would imagine this altitude, so lofty from a human perspective, to effect any significant improvement in one's relation to the sun and its warmth. In short, even the summers here in the Engadine can be insanely cold. For some time following my arrival the weather was most unpleasant, as I have previously reported, more volatile than any lowlander can readily comprehend. I reckon my July a loss on balance, but so far August is better, much better. Today is my twelfth consecutive day of truly *good health* and *high spirits*. And although on this day I have often been haunted by melancholy memories and strange visions, I have also experienced moments of great joy. More, I have shuddered with upwellings of strength sufficient to celebrate them all, to affirm my lows as well as my highs and thereby to turn *all* moods to *my* benefit. Sometimes, you know, I can almost imagine myself a magician in this regard.

But, really, you should see me. Despite my usual bouts of illness, I am as fit as I have ever been. Every morning one egg yolk and a biscuit with tea for breakfast; meat and macaroni for lunch; every evening polenta (in the tradition of the hardy Italian *contadini*—farmers and peasants, you understand), and, once again, egg yolks, a biscuit, and tea. I walk for hours every day, through bright meadows, dark woods, and over rocky hills. I write. Indeed, my thoughts of late are so alive that I feel pregnant with the future. Like a woman, a storm-cloud, or a blooming fig-tree. Sometimes I fear I will burst before I am ripe. But I conserve my resources with an eye toward my highest and best productivity. In the evening after reading I sit in the dark for at least one hour to allow my eyes to rest. This calm before bed has the additional benefit of inducing sound sleep and pleasant dreams.

But this last word reminds me of the unusual dream that disturbed my sleep early this morning. It recalled father and poor brother Joseph, only I was the pair of them, and somehow my birth was also my death, and my death my birth. ~~And~~ Or, well, enough of that! As I say, I am very well, despite the occasional black mood or strange dream. This is how it goes with me, as you know by now as well as I. I trust you forgive me my unconventional life. To live and work efficiently with this flawed machine of a body, I have to be hard on myself. With love,

Your F.

(Please pass the enclosed note to Lisbeth)

***

My dear sister,

A few words to you, dear Lama, to let you know that I am well, and to request a proper note from you whenever you have the time to catch me up on the latest with yourself and our circle of acquaintances.

Today, friends and family have been much on my mind, most every one of them long passed out of my life. And here I sit atop my mountain, alone... I have been thinking of R.W., too—that old wizard of a man! Just now I recall Bayreuth: the '76 inaugural. What a fiasco! But I really was at the end of my tether. What could I do? I could not breathe. I simply had to leave. Of course I enjoyed what I heard of the rehearsals. The 'Ring' truly is an astounding achievement. Even today I still love the man's music—as much as I loathe it too. But the crowds! The mindless sight-seers, the *poseurs* and 'educated' philistines! The heat! And the long evenings! No: I could not see. I could not think. I could not *live*.

But why rehearse these gloomy matters? Sorrento did me good—no matter what my friends thought at the time. The south liberated me! Did I not finally break with Schopenhauer there? Did I not discover my *free* spirit? True, these were the days of my last contact with R.W. I admit I was anxious and uncomfortable in his presence. But he had possessed such a commanding hold on me, a hold I simply had to break, having finally seen through his actor's *façade* to the Romantic corruption rooted in his heart. And the maudlin religious tenor of his talk! So disingenuous too! Really, to have accomplished all he had accomplished in the spirit of the Greeks—and then to speak like a Christian, like a Catholic even!

I was in need of R.W. when I found him, or so I thought. Someone above me. Someone to inspire me to seek a path beyond myself. But he turned out not to be the man I thought he was, and my fever for him nearly did me in. Has it not taken years to repair the damage his music did to my nerves?! No, he was not the man to lead me beyond myself. Now I understand that I, and *I alone*, am that man. I am my own self-overcoming. I say 'Yes!' not only to my present self, but also to the man I have been and will yet become.

But I am sorry. I should not burden you with my thoughts. Your life will be easier if you can say in all honesty that you do not know what I am about. For someday everyone will eagerly tell you that I am mad. And perhaps I am—mad with wisdom! But enough. My best to you, dear Lisbeth, and, as always, my love.

Your brother

The professor read these letters over again, then folded them up and laid them aside. He wondered whether to post them. Perhaps he should compose them afresh, omitting all the revealing, and potentially disturbing, content. No need to upset his mother with reminders of her departed husband and child. And as for Elizabeth, she was still close with members of the Wagner crowd, and he deplored her bad habit of exploiting her intimacy with himself to acquire and maintain cachet among others. She doled out enticing scraps of information to curious acquaintances; and whether her facts were accurate or not seemed not always to matter, so long as they were such as to hold interest, and even better if they reflected well on her. He did not want her suggesting to others that she had any special insight into the latest trends of his thinking, for she had trouble comprehending his thoughts even when he explained them to her, which he had long since given up doing. Besides, she usually did not approve the little she did understand. Therefore she simply wished away whole parts of his philosophy, even suggested to others he hadn't really meant this or that idea he had published, or that he'd secretly intended to imply a contrary, and more socially acceptable, thought. It really was infuriating. But what could he do? She was his sister, and he loved her. Well, he reasoned, he could do what he usually did these days: leave her out of it, and politely discourage her interest. Similarly, he did not want her peddling gossip about his regrets relating to his actions or intentions in the dissolution of his relationship with Wagner, even if only 'discreetly,' as she no doubt would insist she was doing. On this point he was firm. People could read his books for themselves; no need to trust his sister's word about his philosophy. But as he could not explain to the relevant parties his personal relations to Wagner, his feelings and frustrations about his involvement with him, he thought it best to drape a veil over these matters, at least until he judged it appropriate to reveal the facts himself.

His friendship with Wagner had begun to deteriorate before the inaugural Bayreuth festival, even as he composed a long essay, 'Richard Wagner in Bayreuth,' in honor of the man. The situation paralleled the earlier episode of his writing his celebrated 'Schopenhauer as Educator' while revising his estimation of the merit of Schopenhauer's philosophy. He later judged these two essays early examples of his talent for self-overcoming. In both instances he adopted, if only unconsciously, the role of a son rebelling against his father. Yet his was not the mindless rebellion of immature adolescence, but rather the revolt of one who must remove himself from the shadow cast by a dominant influence in order to step into the light of his own greatness.

The Wagners' departure from Tribschen added physical separation to the developing intellectual divide. Bayreuth being some distance from Basel, it was inconvenient to visit even on long weekends. In his isolation from Wagner the young professor's incipient reservations about the man and his music expanded into serious doubts and, in some cases, resolute disagreements. He recorded critical observations in his notebooks. Wagner was too much an actor, his works too theatrical, which smacked of disingenuousness; his music as well as his narratives tended, like Schopenhauer's philosophy, toward fantastical escapism, despair, and life-denial; he was too domineering, in his person as well as in his compositions; he could neither brook rivals nor approach potential peers with generosity of spirit. This last trait presented no particular problem for men who were followers and courtiers by nature. But the professor was a higher type than this, and even in the early phase of his career he suspected as much.

His complaints about the atmosphere surrounding the Bayreuth festival, as rehearsed in his letter to his sister, were genuine as far as they went. But underlying all else was the necessity of liberation from the constraints of the influence of 'The Master.' His departure from Bayreuth appeared to others, and even to himself at times, as a flight *from* something; but in truth he was rushing *toward* something, toward his freedom, his future, and ultimately of course toward himself.

At Bayreuth his friend Malwida von Meysenbug invited him to pass the winter with her and several others in a villa in southern Italy. As he had recently been granted a sabbatical from teaching due to an increase in the frequency and intensity of his attacks, he accepted the invitation and arranged to stay in Sorrento, near Naples, for several months of physical recuperation and emotional and intellectual regeneration. When he wrote to his sister that the south had liberated him, and that he had discovered his free spirit there, he was referring to this winter in Sorrento. While there he wrote the bulk of his first thoroughly philosophical work, *Human, All Too Human*, to which he affixed the subtitle, 'A Book for Free Spirits.' The book was an expression of his final break with Schopenhauer and Wagner, in style and substance a radical departure from his *Birth of Tragedy*. This latter work was still so popular with his and Wagner's friends that they were dismayed by the new direction of his thought. He regarded the book as another expression of his self-overcoming, through which he ascended in stages ever closer to himself. To others, however, to the majority possessed of a narrow vision and middling aspirations, he appeared mercurial and unfaithful to himself. But these types understood and approved only the now, the familiar and comfortable; they avoided the strangeness and pain of change and Becoming. But, as the professor well knew, their fear inhibited growth. Such timidity was not for him, for as mightily as he strove to affirm the past and the present, he always had his mind's eye trained on the future, which would after all eventually become present and past as well.

The Wagners vacationed in Sorrento for a time while the professor was there, a short walk from Meysenbug's villa. The two men spent a few hours together, but from the mutual tension and reserve it was evident that their intimacy was no more. The professor sent Wagner a copy of his new book when it appeared, but, as Cosima recorded in her diary, her husband read only very little of the work. He could not endure the radical skepticism at the center of the professor's new methodology; the anti-metaphysical, and, more specifically, the anti-Schopenhauerian tenor of his new ideas; his relentless determination to burrow under, expose, and uproot the presuppositions of all that Wagner held dear—ideas which he had assumed the professor, too, had cherished. Of course he had, formerly. But, as always in his life, he felt the urge to grow, to expand, to create himself anew; and as he often insisted, growth and expansion demand sacrifice, creation requires annihilation. The professor sacrificed his past to his future self, annihilating his relationship with Wagner in the process. After Sorrento, the two friends, so like father and son, never met again.

The professor remained a full six months in Sorrento. So occupied were his days with pleasant diversions and sustained intellectual labor that he managed often to put the break with Wagner out of mind. And although he suffered his usual nervous fits, the temperate climate and the company of friends provided hours of relief. When he returned to Basel, however, burdened by the resumption of his teaching duties, the old gloom descended again, darkening his mood, and his ailments and attacks grew ever more severe, ever crueler, more viciously incapacitating. His eyesight deteriorated to the point that his doctor insisted he abandon reading and writing altogether. He would go blind, he warned. His sister rushed to Basel to care for him, reading to him and taking dictation. His friend Overbeck would have liked to help, and he assisted whenever he could; but he was not often available, for he had recently become engaged.

The professor had befriended Franz Overbeck when the latter arrived in Basel to join the faculty of theology and rented a room in his building. The two men met by chance in the hall one morning, exchanged introductions and pleasantries, and each immediately recognized the other for a sympathetic soul. Intellectually they were worlds apart, but Overbeck's faith was not the thoughtless conviction of a simpleminded believer. In fact, he published a work soon after his arrival in which he critically analyzed Christian theology as a sophisticated system alien to the primitive beliefs of Christ and his disciples. His central thesis amounted to a repudiation of centuries of Christian doctrine. This radical streak in Overbeck's nature endeared him to Fritz, incorrigibly nonconformist himself.

But quite apart from their intellectual relationship, the two men were particularly compatible as character types. Overbeck was quiet, considerate, urbane, very well educated, and intellectually and emotionally empathetic. He understood Fritz even when he could not agree with him; and he was happy to adopt the role as needed of conversationalist, devil's advocate, or sympathetic ear. The two men regularly dined in Overbeck's room, took walks and played piano together. And whenever Fritz was ill, as he so often was, Overbeck served as his primary caretaker.

Unfortunately, when Fritz fell ill following his return from Sorrento, the flurry of activity accompanying Overbeck's engagement prevented him from nursing his friend as regularly as he had previously been accustomed to do. In time Fritz came to admire Overbeck's wife, Ida; and he visited the couple many times over the years, often staying in their home when he came to town. But the initial report of their engagement had dispirited him. He had been severed from yet another friend, he thought, and at one of the lowest points of his life. Indeed, this was the period of his most precarious physical decline, a three-year period that culminated in his permanent retirement from the university. Franz and Ida did what they could to help, and Elizabeth was tireless in her devotion. But in the end there was nothing to be done. The professor was determined to take his health and future into his own hands. And thus began the solitary itinerant life that brought him eventually to Sils-Maria.

***

Still undecided whether to post the letters to his mother and sister, but feeling a pressing need to unburden his heart and mind to a friend, the professor took up a pencil and a clean sheet of paper and wrote to Overbeck.

Dear, dear friend,

So here am I still on my mountain, thinking my high-altitude thoughts, so strange to the inhabitants of the lowlands below, who gawk at my ideas as if they were staring up at fantastic figures metamorphosing in the clouds. Yes, I am something of an artist, am I not? On my palette are colors, on my canvas textures, which no painter hitherto has so much as imagined. How then can I expect the earthbound hordes of tasteless spectators to appreciate my work? I cannot, and therefore I do not. But you, dear friend, you always understand me!

When in my previous note I wrote that I was longing for death—well, that was true at the time. All too true. How miserable the weeks I spent in bed here, the electrified atmosphere exciting my nerves with charges beyond their capacity. I flopped and jerked like a frog's leg in Galvani's laboratory! And afterwards, oh afterwards, how profoundly I collapsed! How absolute the unconsciousness! At times I really did think I would die—and I was happy for it.

But now at last my sun is high again, shining boldly, proudly, cheerfully—yes, *cheerfully*—in the zenith of its orbit. At long last I am bright! This is not to say, you understand, that I am now without my pain and suffering. No, these two demons—I know this now—shall be my lifelong companions. They are my *best* training partners, the noble enemies whose opposition incites me to my own nobility of power. In short, my pain and my suffering are planks in the bridge to my future, to my greatest health and highest happiness, the bridge, in a word, to *myself*. If the last five years of my hard life have taught me anything, they have taught me at least this much. And thus I overleap the summit of my suffering by descending into the abysm of my pain.

Today I am feeling especially well—as perhaps you infer from my tone—and this not despite the fact that a melancholy vein runs through the marble of my mind, but rather *because* of it. Purity is a weakness, you know, a laziness. An organism grows strong by having to contend with internal elements of corruption. Therefore I say 'Yes!' to this day, its shadows as well as its sun. And as this day is the offspring of every previous yesterday, and in turn the progenitor of every subsequent tomorrow—since this is so, I say 'Yes!' to *all time.*

The professor dropped his pencil, neglecting to sign the note, so excited had he become in writing. The 'Yes!' he described in the concluding paragraph thrilled through his body and mind, stimulating every muscle and nerve. He leapt from his seat and jumped into the air several times, pushing off the floor with the balls of his feet while keeping his legs straight, knees locked, his arms outstretched and uplifted. He spun around in circles. He wept and sang.

"Eternity," he sang, or rather chanted, spinning and weeping. "Eternity! Yes! Eternity! I love you, O eternity!"

This behavior persisted for a full five minutes. He worked himself into a sweat. Then, as he calmed down, he paced the room, rapidly at first, then ever more slowly until he stopped altogether and stood in place. When finally he relaxed, he removed his handkerchief from his pocket and dried his cheeks and wiped his eyes, fastened an undone button of his shirt, then crossed the room and put an ear to the door to check whether he had disturbed anyone in the house. Hearing neither movement nor voices beyond, he returned to his chair and sat down before his letter to Overbeck. He picked up his pencil and concentrated to still his trembling hand, then he wrote in farewell:

Dear friend, how I long to see you and your lovely wife. I shall make a point of visiting soon, on my word.

Your wild friend, F.

The professor smiled at his signature, anticipating his friend's delight upon reading it. As analytically staid as Overbeck was, he appreciated Fritz's mad Dionysian tendencies. Appreciated them, that is, until finally they terrified him, as they did some seven years later when he received a postcard from the professor, who was staying in Turin, Italy. His scrawl was barely legible, the substance of his note incomprehensible, and the signature read, simply, "Dionysus." When he heard that same day from common friends who had also received disturbing notes, Overbeck posted a letter to Turin. Then, considering the potential severity of the situation, he rushed to the station and boarded a train for Italy. When he finally located the house in which his friend was staying, the exasperated landlord informed him that the professor had been acting erratically for days, banging on the piano at all hours, rearranging the furniture in his room and removing the paintings from the walls, singing and shouting for no apparent reason, refusing to eat then consuming more than his allotted share of the kitchen's food. Then one morning he collapsed in a nearby piazza, crying, kicking, and spitting. Raving. When they brought him home and returned him to his room, he settled down and slept for twenty hours. Since then he'd been cycling through periods of calm, distress, terror, mania, and outright unhinged madness.

The landlord indicated to Overbeck the way to the professor's room at the far end of the second-floor hallway, but he refused to escort him there. He would remain downstairs beside the open front door—in case of emergency, he said; because he is terrified, Overbeck thought. And why not? Thumps, cries, and whimpering whispers echoed through the hallway above, which was dark and otherwise quiet. For a moment Overbeck was possessed by an urge to flee the house and catch the first train home. But of course he could never abandon his friend. Therefore he steeled himself and climbed the stairs, then crept down the hall toward the professor's closed door. As he approached, stepping lightly, he heard a distinct voice within the room, speaking casually in Italian, as if an average citizen were addressing a friend over lunch.

"Are we content?" Overbeck recognized the professor's voice.

"I am god." This took him aback. He froze in place, leaned in and put his ear to the door.

Footsteps. Mumbling and heavy breathing.

Overbeck nervously tapped at the door with the tips of his fingers.

"I am god." The professor spoke more urgently now, raising his voice, but he did not answer the door.

Now Overbeck knocked on the center of the door hard with his knuckles, then stepped back and hung his head, staring at his shoes and shuffling his feet. A minute passed, or more, during which time no sound whatever emerged from the room. He finally resolved to act when he heard a shattering of glass, or of china, within. Clinching his teeth, he stepped forward, reached out and turned the doorknob, pushing lightly against the brass handle. As the door swung open he entered the room to find the professor in rumpled clothes with tousled hair, standing erect and gesticulating as if he were conducting an orchestra.

"I am god," he repeated, this time in the grandiloquent manner of a monarch issuing an official proclamation to an assembled throng of admiring subjects.

"Behold: I created this world of masks and appearances!"

The expression on the professor's face was unnerving. He seemed actually to address a presence before him, gazing unblinkingly into the eyes of an invisible being—god or man, who could say? He appeared blissful. Then he began slowly to dance, to turn, singing softly to himself a single word,

"Yes, yes, yes."

As he spun he looked at Overbeck standing in the doorway, but he did not perceive him. His eyes turned away as he continued to revolve.

"Yes, yes, yes."

Overbeck looked on mesmerized, horrified, sobbing. Minutes passed, or seconds; he could not measure. Finally he caught the professor's eyes, and they flared with a flash of recognition.

"Yes, yesss… Oh, no! Overbeck?!"

He was embarrassed and confused, lost, utterly absent from himself.

"But why are *you* here?! Where *are* we?! Who—"

And with that his face sank, his arms fell limp at his side, and he stumbled forward and collapsed into Overbeck's arms, quivering, weeping, helplessly insane.

3:00 pm – 5:30 pm

The professor addressed an envelope to Overbeck in Basel, sealed the letter inside, then crossed the room and slipped it into the right pocket of his jacket, which hung on the back of his door. He would let the letters to his mother and sister sit for a day. Withdrawing his pencil from his left pocket, he pressed its tip with his thumb, then replaced it and reached inside to feel for his notebook. Confident that his pencil was sharp and his notebook safely in place, he stepped over to the bureau to prepare for his walk to Lake Silvaplana. His twelfth consecutive visit to the area.

"A high noon," he thought. "The midday of my high-spirited walking and thinking among these mountains and lakes." He pictured the pyramidal stone on the shore, imagined it awaiting his arrival, waiting since the ice retreated, ancient, prehistoric, timeless.

Rolling up his shirtsleeves, he washed his hands in the water bowl, shook them off and ran them through his hair. Then he leaned forward and combed his wet hair back while studying his features in the mirror. His forehead was furrowed with the lines of a thinker; his brows projected like granite crags overshadowing his brown eyes, which appeared to focus on a point just beyond the spatio-temporal world; his thick moustache obscured the whole of his mouth but the center of a soft bottom lip; his jaws were firm if somewhat fleshy; his elegant nose flared at the nostrils, and on its bridge his old saber scar caught the light. He smiled at himself, intentionally, his method for inducing a good mood. Then he drew up still closer to the mirror and stared into his own eyes, focusing to catch in the reflected pupils the reflection of himself staring into his own eyes.

Infinite regress, he thought; then he spoke aloud a single word, "Yes!"

After drying his face and hands, he took his jacket from the door, reached into his right pocket to touch his letter to Overbeck, then squeezed his notebook through the fabric of his left pocket. Then leaving his room he descended the stairs and left the house through the front door. Outside on the porch he paused, as was his habit, to observe the Fedacla on the far side of the lawn, the flowering meadows beyond, and Lagrev rising sublime still farther across the valley.

"Yes!" he whispered, to which Herr Durisch, whom he hadn't noticed still working in the yard near the side of the house, replied, "Excuse me, sir?"

Startled, the professor turned and saw his landlord sitting up from his labors, mucky but relaxed, cheerful from hard work in the open air. "Oh, Herr Durisch!" he exclaimed, somewhat embarrassed. "Pardon me, sir. I, I didn't see you there. I was greeting this beautiful afternoon and your lovely Sils landscape. Ha! It's foolish, I know."

"No, sir, not at all," Durisch replied, smiling. "I understand you completely. We really are fortunate to have wound up in such a place. God knows how! But it does one's heart and head good, and the body too." And he bent over and plunged his trowel into the dirt.

"Indeed it does, Herr Durisch," the professor spoke while gazing up at the sun, still high but declining toward the peaks to the west of Maloja. "Indeed it does."

Durisch turned to look at the professor over his shoulder, and said, "So you're off to Silvaplana, I suppose. We'll see you later, then. And a good afternoon to you, sir."

"And happy gardening to you, sir," the professor replied, and he stepped from the porch and crossed the lawn on the stones laid out in the grass.

The post office stood a few doors down from the Durisch house on the way to Silvaplana. The professor followed the path along the Fedacla, then turned off to enter the building and hand his letter to the man at the desk inside. The mail would go out tomorrow, he was told, which was fine; he was in no hurry. Then, resuming his walk, he allowed his mind to wander as he scanned the scenery through which he moved. He pictured himself from above, from the sky, a tiny figure, only a speck, a point moving beside the unspooling thread of the river like a line of droplets cast up on the bank by the splashing water. Then looking down at his feet he observed such a droplet spray on the ground and dissolve in a patch of grass before him. He was struck by how large, how solid and durable, he was in comparison. From his subjective point of view he was gigantic and enduring. He was the All. He was everything and his life-span forever. From the perspective of the universe, however, he was a minuscule and fleeting mirage, just barely on the positive side of nothing, a trick of the mind, a puzzle, a question mark.

He conjured the image of a question mark and regarded it as a representation of himself, as in a dream one transposes figures and their proper significations. Then, as if from nowhere, he was overwhelmed by the sense that he had thought this thought before, not a similar thought, but this identical thought; and not in some other place and time, but in this very Here and Now. He slowed his pace and attended to both his internal state and the external surroundings. Yes, he had experienced all this before, the thought in his mind, the associated emotion, the specific posture of his body, the wind in his hair, the warmth caressing his ears and cheeks. Everything. He was certain of it. But this could not be. It made no sense. Right, of course it made no sense, nevertheless... But before he could further analyze his uncanny subjective state, the feeling faded, leaving a dazed, dreamlike sensation in its wake. Then this too passed and he felt normal again. Or, he wondered, had he returned to the usual human state of psychic abnormality? But he was distracted from this new line of inquiry by the sound of a rooster crowing somewhere nearby.

The burst from the rooster reminded him of the crowing he'd heard that morning after waking from his disturbing dream. He stopped and scanned the area but saw no chicken coops. As he was near the outskirts of the village, where many of the local farmers lived, he assumed they kept their animals behind their houses hard against the forested base of Corvatsch. He stood still and listened intently, but he heard only the wind gathering speed on its way across the meadow toward Lake Silvaplana. He sensed his right temple pulsing, but after a moment of concentrated inspection he found that his head did not hurt. Relieved, he walked on, maintaining his bearing north as the Fedacla ran off to the west where it flowed into the lake in the shadow of Mt. Lagrev.

Leaving the houses of Sils behind, he proceeded through the center of the meadow, following the loggers' track toward the southern shore of Silvaplana. The green of the grass among the wildflowers called to mind the expansive fields around his childhood home in the pastorage. The landscape actually was quite different, including even the particular shade of the grass, but as his morning's dream still circulated among his thoughts, the association was irresistible. He pictured the little church, the house, and the happy family within. He pictured his father strolling thoughtfully outdoors, composing sermons in his mind; sitting at his desk, reading and writing; playing the piano, winking, swaying to the music—very much as he now filled his own days. He saw his father speaking from behind a high pulpit, standing before the grave of a deceased parishioner, lying sick and delirious in bed. Then he saw himself weeping at his father's grave, at his brother's grave, and finally at his own grave.

Death. His father's death. His brother's. His own. In his dream they had all been one, but returning also to life. Not as a resurrection, however, nor as a reincarnation. His was no Christian or Platonic dream. He certainly was no Socrates, he thought, sacrificing roosters for liberation from the sickness, the imprisonment, of corporeality. Socrates' pious devotion to Asclepius was a blasphemy against life, against *his own* life, and therefore against *himself*. Socrates was the demon who taught the great 'No!' to life, a lesson learned by Plato, educator in turn of the Christians.

Damn the *Phaedo* and its seductive portrait of the dying Socrates! Damn its immortal soul and lust to escape the cycle of rebirth! Damn its oppositions! The professor preferred Heraclitus's style, neither exploiting nor resolving contrary tendencies, but allowing them to flourish in fecund juxtaposition. He recited to himself a fragment: "Immortals mortals

mortals immortals living the death of those dying the life of those." Here was a labyrinth in which he could happily lose himself, a convoluted and backward-turning lair of a minotaur he could attack and embrace simultaneously!

The professor approached the loggers' heaps of drying wood stacked on the shore of the lake, their bright little ribbons fluttering in the wind, then he turned to follow the branching path to the right, winding along the bank toward the eastern shoreline. Ahead in the distance stood long, high, inclined rows of pines and larches running up the steep base of Corvatsch. Overlapping layers of emerald green, hunter green, moss green, and lime. The sun in the west shone on the needles and leaves, which responded with flares of shimmering light projected before the voids between the slender trunks and branches. The water to his left slapped and slurped against the low bank, massaging the pebbles settled among the undulating reeds beneath the surface.

"Twenty-five hundred years," he thought, "yet still no one has caught up with Heraclitus. Plato in his *Theaetetus* had the sense to acknowledge radical Becoming, but he lacked the decency, the intellectual honesty, to stop there. Something induced him to postulate Being in addition. Fear? Of uncertainty? Of death? Yes, ignorance, suffering, and death. And so the story has proceeded ever since. Even old Schopenhauer, the first forthright atheist among us Germans, the first moreover to dethrone Reason from her temple and recognize the prior rights of instinct and will, even he succumbed to the lure of Being and preached the gospel—or, rather, the *bad* news—of the denial of life for Being's sake. And, oh, didn't Wagner turn out to be such a dutiful little catechumen! He *said* 'tragedy,' but in the end he *did* Christianity. Even the maestro reached out to touch the hem of the divine garment, held it to his lips and besought redemption. Oh, the dishonesty! The treachery to oneself! The weakness!"

Now the path running north climbed into the trees above the lake. The shaded coolness was refreshing after the half-hour's walk from the Durisch house. A still silence saturated the forest upon the mountain slope, thick like a presence, heavy but supple, undisturbed, accentuated even, by pattering wings and treble bursts of birdsong, the rumbling bass of insects sounding among fallen leaves. The professor paused beside a small cascade, sat on a stone and sipped cold water from his hands. Then he turned and looked between the trees at the lake below, azure capped with flashes of white, like a noon sky flecked with cloud, a mountain crowned with ice. He embraced his knees and inhaled his surroundings: the colors, the scents, breathing them in; the air, the breeze, infusing his lungs; the beauty pervading his heart; the energy exciting his nerves; the exuberance galvanizing his limbs, welling up through his body entire. Oh, the cheerfulness! The good will! The joy!

The professor shuddered and bolted to his feet, leapt over the falls and sprinted until the path leveled off along the plateau. Then as suddenly as he had darted from his seat, he stopped, stood still to catch his breath, then resumed his walk at a moderate pace, interlocking his fingers behind his back. He whistled. He hummed a tune. He called to a bird in a tree. Then he called again and the bird replied, or so he imagined, and immediately he thought of the wood-bird's song from

Wagner's *Siegfried*, reprised in *Götterdämmerung* just prior to Siegfried's death. "Ah, the twilight of the gods," he sighed. "Would that that old wizard had seen still further than this! But he was only an artist after all, no match as a man for his art. Certainly no match as a thinker. Therefore it's no surprise that he too was caught in the deceitful web of Being, the lie of God. Twilight of the gods, indeed! Would that he had known that God is dead!"

The path declined on its crooked way back down toward the lake, where it twisted along the bank approaching the hulking pyramidal stone, alien in its strangeness, mystic in its allure. The professor could already sense on his skin the vibrations cast off in radiating waves from the stone's ancient face.

"Where are the minds unclouded by the storm of God?" he asked himself, descending toward the lake, emerging from the trees. "Where are the clear-sky minds, crisp and bright as *this* sky illumined by *this* sun? And oh the delusions that hide behind the divine name! Substance, form, essence, thing, ego, atom, truth—so many synonyms of Being, so many masks of God. Everyone wants to be given something, therefore they love the gift-giver, the giver of meaning and of the purpose of existence in particular. Lacking the gift for giving, of themselves to themselves, they beg and take from others, others whom they call their priests, or their gods. Where is the man who bestows himself upon himself, receives himself from his own hands, the man who creates his own gift of meaning and purpose?"

Returned to level ground beside the lake, the professor proceeded along the winding path, water to his left, splashing, forest to his right, whispering, a numinous sky overhead, and the stone rising up before him in the distance. He observed it as he approached, a dense, broad-based mass anchored in the soil, its apex a repetition of the mountain peaks nearby, for ages reposing beside the flowing falls, whose liquid circular emanations diffused into the lake, one after another, moment to moment, hour to hour, for days on end, for months, years, centuries, millennia... for as long as there had been mountain, falls, and lake. The tips of his fingers tingled at the thought, his right trapezius contracted, his heart quickened.

Finally drawing close to the stone, the professor was overcome. It seemed somehow an externalized fragment of his spirit, and the experience of this twosomeness sliced into his heart. And now he stood beside the stone, beside himself, ecstatic. He rested his back against the stone's broad back, closed his eyes and watched his thoughts explode and fly apart as diamond fragmentations, then contract into a single rotating point and disappear. His mind went blank. He was nothing but his breath, which was air, which was the sky.

For several minutes he reclined upright against the stone. But as it was his habit to walk at least as far as the meadow on the northern shore before returning to linger on the sedimental outcrop between the stone and the waterfall, he opened his eyes, righted himself, then followed the path around the bend into the sun-drenched field.

The distance from the stone was calming, a restorative respite from the nervous excitations induced by its proximity. The meadow displayed its flowing rows of red, ochre, and dark green, interspersed with yellow and white. The professor drew these colors into himself, the flowers' scents, the warmth and the wind too; he absorbed the tranquil atmosphere through eyes, ears, nose, skin, and steady, deep inhalations. Soon he eased into a tranquil state himself. Then kneeling down he picked a daisy, twirled it between his fingers. The petals spun like the hands of a clock. Then he turned to observe the course of the waterfall that tumbled down amid the trees to his left, emptying into the lake beside the stone. He peered up toward the highest visible point of the cascade's course, where the water spilled over a ridge of stone in surging bursts, then he tracked the plummeting tide's descent as he walked from the meadow and returned around the bend toward the stone and the waterfall's base.

Stepping down onto the curving shore beside the falls, the stone a looming presence in his peripheral vision, the professor watched the water leap from behind the trees and course into the lake. The chaos of overlapping ripples near the shore progressively resolved into ordered patterns of circular waves radiating far out on the water. He dropped his daisy and watched it bob away, pushed along before the concentrically expanding rollers, which wrinkled the surface on and on until eventually they slowed, diminished, then dissolved. His eye ran out into the lake along with them, skimming the surface of the water; and when the waves disappeared he looked beyond them, past the southern shore of the lake and across the Sils meadows, picking up the distant outline of the mountains beyond Maloja, tracing their inclines up to their peaks, which pointed into the canopy sky at a lone white cloud moving in his direction. He watched the cloud as it drifted toward him, over the meadows, over the lakes, then finally passed right over his head and arced away toward the horizon beyond.

Full circle, he thought. A revolving series of phases running out and away then cycling back again. The meadows, the lakes, the sky: earth, water, and air. The endless natural cycle of the elements' interblending transmutations. And fire? Ah, but fire suffuses the whole, he reflected. The fiery river of energy that fuels every transformation, which *is* every transformation, chemical, mechanical, physical, psychic, spiritual. From matter to mind, the great chain of Being is an apparition, this world an empire of hallucinatory figures dancing in the flaming waves on the river of Becoming.

Standing between the waterfall and the stone, a point on the curve of the elements' fiery wheel of transmutation, the professor reviewed his day, which had been marked throughout by memories of his past and premonitions of his future. In this single day, he thought, the entirety of my life is mirrored, the whole in the part, the *ever* in the *moment*. The people, the events, the thoughts, moods, and emotions he had relived, his alternating periods of sickness and health, suffering and joy—all this had long since passed. Long since. Yet somehow the whole of it seemed still to be with him, as a part of him, *as* him. "And who would I be, now," he asked himself, "if not for them, then?" And in that moment he saw himself, in his present Now, as a past Then in relation to himself in some future Now. "And who will I be, then, if not for myself, now?"

His past, present, and future were bound together in a knot, his future conditioned by his present conditioned by his past, this past conditioned by his present conditioned by his future. Causality and will, the transfer of energy and the propagation of influence, spread out in every direction from every point, an entangled web in which every moment was bound up with every other moment.

With these thoughts revolving in his mind, the professor advanced toward the stone, stepped onto the path and walked right up beside it, from which vantage he observed the mountains across the valley, the lake, the falls, and the skin of the stone itself, against which he rested his left hand. He thought then of his father, dying before he could know his son as a man, before as a man he could know his father. Perhaps it was for the best; they would not have understood each other. Still, he had been deprived, and the pain of loss was real, and in a way always present. He recalled an autobiographical essay he had written as a child, in which he compared the death of his father to a tree's losing its crown of leaves to blight. From such trees the birds depart, life flees, and eventually they waste away. Just so, upon the death of his father his family was bereft, and joy gave way to grief and despair. In a later reminiscence he recorded his regret that his father's death had deprived him of the paternal care a son requires on his way to manhood, and had thereby in some sense stunted or perverted his development. Yet he acknowledged that the loss had bestowed on him the gift of a serious, contemplative nature. He lamented and affirmed his father's death simultaneously.

"And now, too," he thought, "even now I cannot deny the harm the loss of my father inflicted on me, a harm no doubt manifesting still in numerous vulnerabilities and vices, my poor health in particular; and yet I affirm the pain, the suffering, and, yes, even the early death, for all this made me the man I am today, and I must affirm myself as I am or resign myself to my own death, a living death of life-denial, which father would not have wanted for me, and for which he would no doubt have given his life, good man that he was.

"Ah," he mused, "and is this not the tragedy of existence? Life comes only from death, creation from annihilation, joy from pain. Not as a cosmological necessity, as old Plato would have it, but rather for those with the power to extract the good from the bad, to overcome themselves into their highest height by way of their deepest abyss. The rare ones. The affirmers of life. The Yes-sayers."

The triumphs and losses of his life now flashed before his mind's eye in recurring cycles of progress and reversal, joy and suffering, grief and celebration: an innocent heart embraced by familial love, at play in flowering fields; piano keys and bright chords; his father's winking eye; spring; dawn; the midday sun—followed by dusk, always by dusk and midnight; his sister's wailing, "father is dead," weeping in the dark; the untimely death of baby Joseph; his mother's anguished tears; school days with Deussen, friend Deussen; studiousness and drunkenness, reflection and rebellious adolescence; Leipzig, Ritschl, and Rohde, his lost twin; the jubilant surprise of the call to Basel; the loneliness, the drudgery, the debilitating migraines and blindness; Wagner and the sublimity of friendship; the profundity of separation;

Overbeck and enduring attachment; self-imposed exile, wandering among shadows, *as* a shadow. The fear of madness. Fear of death. All these embodiments of emotions and moods, corporeal expressions of spiritual states; all the joy, all the longing, all the many sorrows, and all the splendors of happiness: all this together was his life, a river of flux forever bending away from itself and curving back again, the circulating eddies on its surface microcosmic images of the whole.

With his hand still resting on the stone, absorbing its mystic vibrations, the professor watched a wave materialize from the agitated ripples at the base of the falls. Like every identical preceding and subsequent wave, it expanded and rolled across the lake, a swelling arc at one with the water yet distinct as an individual, an image of a moment moving in the womb of eternity, diffusing the Now into Forever and drawing it back again, the respiration of life into death, death into life. The lake rocked with amplifying circular undulations, heaving out against its banks, contracting into its deepest center.

"Yes," he thought, "all things pass away forever, but forever returns, time returns, and therefore all things return, too. Forever." And this thought bestowed on him words, words and an accompanying mood, as a gift of thanks, as a child might thank his parents on his own birthday; and he in turn bestowed the words on his thought, as a gift of welcome, a gift of return, a moment returning as it had before, as it would again, and again, forever. He spoke the words aloud, spoke to the lakes, to the meadows and mountains, to the sky, to the stone, to himself, yes, to himself and to his own frenzied heart:

"Was *that* life?" he said. "Well then, once more! And once more! And yes, Yes, YES!"

***

Later, walking back to the Durisches' house, the professor cycled between profound moments of grave silence and Dionysian flights of furious abandon. He plodded with his head down, hands behind his back. Then quickening his pace he shook and laughed and wept from joy, sang nonsense tunes and spoke in broken rhymes.

When finally he returned to his room, before washing or lying down, he withdrew his notebook and pencil from his jacket pocket, sat down at the table under the window, and wrote a long note. He headed the entry,

"The new *heavy weight*: the Eternal Recurrence of the Same."

And beneath the note he wrote,

"Sils-Maria: 6000 feet above the sea, and higher still above all human things!"

THE END

AUTHOR'S NOTE

This is a work of biographical fiction. I have altered or omitted some minor details in service of the narrative, generally for the sake of economy. For instance, contrary to my account, a friend invited Nietzsche to meet Wagner, and the two young men went together to the Brockhaus residence. (Wagner did in fact request the meeting with Nietzsche, and under the circumstances as related in my narrative.) For the most part, however, I have kept to the salient facts of Nietzsche's life and experiences. All the background biographical episodes—Fritz's childhood dream anticipating his brother's death, his visit to the brothel, his struggle with the tailor's delivery-man, the stranger directing him to Sils, to list just a few of several examples—actually happened. The three scenes of the professor's breakdown (presented here as foreshadowings) are also factual, or based on facts, including even the words that Overbeck hears him speak in his room in Turin, which I adapt from one of the last letters Nietzsche wrote, in which he informs a former Basel colleague that he roams the city speaking thus to random people. The story of Fritz spilling pebbles into the old man's umbrella is factual too, but in reality Nietzsche was the man with the umbrella and the children of Sils were the culprits.

The letters throughout are fictionalized versions of Nietzsche's originals. I have of course invented the dialogue and internal monologues, though in doing so I have made every effort to capture the spirit of Nietzsche's personality and thought.

The most thorough biography of Nietzsche in English is, presently, *Friedrich Nietzsche*, by Curtis Cate. However, Daniel Blue's *The Making of Friedrich Nietzsche* provides by far the most reliable account of Nietzsche's youth up to his move to Basel in 1869; and when Mr. Blue completes the other volumes in the series, his work will stand alone as the definitive English-language biography of Nietzsche.*

Translated selections of Nietzsche's letters may be found in two different versions of *Selected Letters of Friedrich Nietzsche*, an older version edited by Oscar Levy and translated by Anthony Ludovici, and a more recent version edited and translated by Christopher Middleton. *Nietzsche: A Self-Portrait from His Letters*, edited and translated by Peter Fuss and Henry Shapiro, is slight but enjoyable. Of particular interest are the reminiscences of Nietzsche's friends and acquaintances collected in *Conversations with Nietzsche*, edited by Sander Gilman and translated by David Parent.

---

* My thanks to Daniel Blue for calling my attention to errors of fact in an early draft of this book. All remaining factual inaccuracies are either intentional or the result of my own ignorance.

www.ingramcontent.com/pod-product-compliance
Lightning Source LLC
Chambersburg PA
CBHW021128300426
44113CB00006B/343